INFLECTION POINTS

INFLECTION POINTS

How to Work and Live with Purpose

Matt Spielman

WILEY

Published by John Wiley & Sons, Inc., Hoboken, New Jersey.
Published simultaneously in Canada.

For general information on our other products and services or for technical support, please contact our Customer Care Department within the United States at (800) 762-2974, outside the United States at (317) 572-3993 or fax (317) 572-4002.

Wiley also publishes its books in a variety of electronic formats. Some content that appears in print may not be available in electronic formats. For more information about Wiley products, visit our web site at www.wiley.com.

Library of Congress Cataloging-in-Publication Data:

Names: Spielman, Matt, author.
Title: Inflection points : how to work and live with purpose / Matt Spielman.
Description: Hoboken, New Jersey : Wiley, [2022] | Includes index.
Identifiers: LCCN 2022007593 (print) | LCCN 2022007594 (ebook) | ISBN 9781119887386 (cloth) | ISBN 9781119887409 (adobe pdf) | ISBN 9781119887393 (epub)
Subjects: LCSH: Satisfaction. | Success.
Classification: LCC BF515 .S65 2022 (print) | LCC BF515 (ebook) | DDC 152.4/2—dc23/eng/20220303
LC record available at https://lccn.loc.gov/2022007593
LC ebook record available at https://lccn.loc.gov/2022007594

COVER DESIGN: PAUL MCCARTHY
COVER ART: © GETTY IMAGES | AERIALPERSPECTIVE IMAGES

SKY10033990_033022

This book is dedicated to those who want to get more out of each day.

CONTENTS

Contents

FOREWORD

Matt Spielman and I met in 1997 in one of the first meaningful exchanges I ever had over email. I had been accepted to business school, found an apartment, and was looking for a roommate. He, in turn, had recently been admitted and was looking for a place to live.

Not long after, I remember sitting on the steps of Harvard Business School's Baker Library with Matt in the days before our first year. We looked out onto the sparkling Charles River and wondered aloud where the journey we were about to embark upon would take us.

A few years ago, my career hit a bump in the road. I had left an investment partnership and was struggling to figure out what would come next. I tried taking a step back to ponder the existential question of my "why," but I couldn't figure out the answer. I began wondering if, as Matt describes, I had been living a professional life of quiet desperation all along.

Without a clear direction, I worked on consulting projects, started a podcast on the side, and day after day racked my brain to find important answers to big questions.

In my quest to move forward, I thought about asking Matt to coach me.

I had some reservations. I had already tried working with coaches in my transition, with little success. Matt had spent years training across disciplines to be a coach. But I questioned what he could offer that those other coaches hadn't.

At the same time, I believed that Matt was in his element as a coach. He has always been driven to help others achieve greatness. He is a dreamer who is in awe of others with vision. He is a feeler in a world of thinkers.

So, I asked if he would take me on as a client.

He said, "No way."

Matt's coaching practice is predicated on listening and reflecting. He believed we were too close for that type of relationship and was concerned it might impact our friendship.

I persisted, he acquiesced, and we decided to give it a shot.

It was one of the best decisions I made on my path.

Matt began our work together from the ground up. Making no assumptions, he began easing into understanding where I was in that moment. He asked thoughtful questions, opened cracks that helped me find barriers in my path, and encouraged me to take small steps of progress.

By the time we created my first action plan, or Game Plan, I had a sense of where I would start heading. Of course, I had understood the importance of having a set of goals and an action plan to achieve them, but it was another thing entirely to visualize *mine* on the page. Matt and his Game Plan System guided me to that point.

When I achieved the goals laid out in the original Game Plan, we co-created another. The same thing happened. I took actions that worked in service of consequential outcomes. Then we co-created another. Each time I reached my objectives, I realized a vision I couldn't see before Matt began working with me.

I can definitively say that Matt's influence was the key inflection point that turned my unclear future into the business that Capital Allocators became. Most importantly, the business flowed from a guiding light of my own "why" that Matt helped me identify, articulate, and foster through the Game Plan System, or GPS.

As for the risk to our friendship, Matt and I are closer than we've ever been. He helped me move toward a potential I knew was within me. And in the 25 years we have been friends, I have never seen him more alive and in the flow than when he is coaching.

In *Inflection Points,* Matt offers not just the "what" of the Game Plan System, but also the "why" and "how" it comes together. He applies that same holistic approach to the book that he does to his coaching practice. It wasn't until I read *Inflection Points* that I understood why my prior attempts with coaching had failed and why Matt's work—although seemingly magical and deeply individualized—was an application of a repeatable process.

Within, Matt describes the tools to help you create flowing moments in your life. He shares the simple-to-incorporate framework that can help make each day count in service of your personal and professional mission. It's a heartfelt and actionable approach that can support many others on their own journey toward, as Matt calls it, an ignited career and an energized life.

I hope you find the wisdom in these pages similarly beneficial in discovering what matters most.

Ted Seides

Host of *Capital Allocators* podcast

January 2022

ACKNOWLEDGMENTS

This book has one author but many people made it happen. First, I would like to thank my beautiful and patient wife, Sharon Fox Spielman; without her support and love, my life would be a shadow of what it is. Adam and Jamie, my boys, put up with me talking about the book, and were there when I sketched out the ACHIEVE model. Thank you for being patient throughout this process.

Next, I would like to acknowledge the folks at Wiley who put considerable effort into this book. These include Bill Falloon, Acquisitions Editor; Purvi Patel, Managing Editor; Samantha Enders, Assistant Editor; Samantha Wu, Editorial Assistant; Pradesh Kumar, Content Refinement Specialist; and Julie Kerr, Copy Editor.

I would also like to thank each of my coaching clients, especially those who believed in me and the approach in the early days. The coaching relationship is a special partnership. There is no coach without the client. You all know who you are. And I thank you.

A special shout-out to Irene McPhail. You gave me a shot with one of your most important corporate relationships.

Thank you, Peter Hazelrigg, my coach of 10 years. You gave me the permission I needed to consider another career path. You hear—and listen to—me, somehow process it, and reflect it back to me. I end our conversations with more clarity, intentionality, and conviction. You are invaluable.

I mentioned I would not share names of clients. However, I would like to thank Ted Seides, who is a client. He was also my roommate in graduate school and knows me as well as almost anybody. We navigate the personal and professional relationship well, and we carve out extra time so we can be former roomies and friends. It feels great to be understood and for someone to see my journey over a 25-year period.

Thank you, Matt Myklusch. While you are a noted author in your own right, you still took the time (where did you find it?) to partner with me to pen several of my first articles for the blog, *Reflection Points*. You helped find my voice, especially early on when I felt like I was shot out of a cannon and had a rush of adrenaline, emotions, and messages.

A special thank you to Laurie Rosenfield. One of your goals as a Chief People Officer was to create a coaching culture within your organization. You brought me in, and we made meaningful strides toward that goal. Thanks to you, we initiated several coaching partnerships across the company.

Thank you, Pete Moore. You taught me the *Win the Day* mantra, which I use and have shared with hundreds of clients. Thank you for also bringing me into your organization and letting me interact with your all-star team.

Dr. Terrence Maltbia, I want to thank you and your team at the Columbia Coaching Certification Program. The rigor of the training has helped fuel the results my clients and I have been able to achieve. And from one university to another, I would like to thank Lauren Murphy, Kristin Fitzpatrick, and the entire team at Harvard Business School's Career & Professional Development Group. Working with CPD and having the opportunity to talk to and coach students and alumni has been one of the most rewarding and meaningful endeavors in my career.

I would like to thank Michael Levin, my writing partner on *Inflection Points*. Without you, this book could not have become a reality. You pushed me and provided encouragement and guidance along the way – especially when it was necessary. You have become a dear friend and I am better off for having gotten to know you through this process.

And finally, I would like to thank my mom, Sherry Bennett Warshauer. You are my mom, my friend, and my inspiration. I look up to you and everything that you have done and everything that you are. I cherish our relationship.

1

WHAT'S YOUR GAME PLAN?

Professional success often conceals a gnawing conflict at one's core—a vague but undeniable sense of lack, that something is askew, off-kilter, or out of place. Even as you pile up accomplishments and accolades, and ascend through the hierarchy of your field, a lingering question resonates in your mind like a ticking clock, or like the steady drip-drip-drip of a faucet as you lie awake in the still of the night: Is this *really* the life I am meant to be living? Is this the life I want? And if it's not, how do I get it?

Henry David Thoreau wrote in 1854 that "the mass of men lead lives of quiet desperation,"[1] locked in a cycle of daily toil interrupted only by brief bouts of leisure that offer a momentary reprieve, but fail to address the frustrating feeling of existential befuddlement.

The world has changed since Thoreau's era, but the observation remains as incisive as ever, and it applies to people from all walks of life, from trades to top-tier executive positions. They know there's more they want to get out of life, whether it's more personal satisfaction, a more meaningful contribution to the world, more community connection, more financial security, more intellectual stimulation, or simply more free time to spend alone or with family. But

---

[1] Thoreau, Henry David. (1854). Walden; or, Life in the Woods.

each time they ponder how to find what it is they want—or to know with certainty *what* they want in the first place—self-doubt blocks action. Is it really possible to have a life and career that is engaging, gratifying, and satisfying?

I know this kind of angst is real because I see it in the clients I coach. I know it's real because I lived under the mantle of quiet desperation myself, for many years, until I realized my purpose in helping others find theirs.

In those days, if you looked at my life from the outside, you might assume I was completely satisfied. At the start of my professional career in 1997, I was working as a salesperson for a prominent investment bank. Although I was working among people much more experienced, I was holding my own, surrounded by all kinds of high achievers. It was a thriving, heady environment, and we were on the rise.

But I wasn't ready to settle in. Something deep inside of me had questions. I felt I could be doing something different. I lacked a sense of personal connection and satisfaction with how I was spending my time. And all around me I observed many others mired in the same grind. They were earning top salaries, but no matter how much they pulled in, the money wasn't rewarding. Some of my colleagues had an irrepressible enthusiasm for the work, but others were, like me, out of place—slogging through each day in anticipation of the next paycheck.

That Thoreau passage was one that came back to me over and over again. Working in that financial ecosystem, I saw a controlled kind of desperation all around me, and I started to understand that I did not belong there. To the contrary, I felt that my real calling in life was to help people escape that kind of desperation. I knew I could help people put their feelings into words, and move those feelings into action. My desire was to be someone who could energize individual lives and careers in a way that would electrify their existence with a clear-eyed passion and a strong intentionality.

My transition from finance to coaching was a long and winding road. I've had many positions in across several industries, and each has been a valuable step to get me to where I am today. There were aspects of my financial career that I enjoyed, but I knew it could not sustain me. A moderately fulfilling life was unacceptable to me. I had to step out of that very traditional job and experience my own setbacks and detours before I found what it was I was looking for. The realization that I had to get out of "the known" and step into "the unknown" was the first stride down what has been a transformative and invigorating path toward the work I do now.

HOW CAN YOU TELL YOU ARE STUCK?

Stasis, stagnation, a sense of being stymied or sedated—these are telltale signs that your mind or soul is crying out for a change. The longing for change usually appears within us before we know how to bring it about—and we rarely know the type of "change" we really need. It's just that *something's gotta give*. But inertia can be an overpowering force that keeps us in place.

We may feel dread and anxiety when we should be feeling anticipation and excitement. Other times, it can be less dramatic. We'll feel a general flatness, and a lack of zest for the things we know should make us happy. You don't have to call it depression (though it may be), but it is the metaphor of living in black and white versus living in color.

In some cases, the problem is that we may set artificially low expectations for ourselves. We just accept that, when it comes to our jobs or our personal lives, there is a certain level of dissatisfaction (the existential toll) that one pays for a stable life and a steady paycheck.

These moments, when you candidly consider whether you are fulfilled, should not be ignored. They are alarm bells that announce it's time for some serious introspection. What do you need? What do you want? And how will you attain it? Only by honest examination can you find the courage to make a change.

5

It's not merely a question of the work you do. While many of my clients seek me out for career guidance, the problem or challenge just as often lies with some other aspect of their life. Some may believe for a lifetime that career is the primary vehicle for self-actualization, only to discover that the intellectual and creative satisfaction they desire comes from a realm outside of the office. Many of my clients are executives who are happy with their career and comfortable in their current role, but seek new means of success or new challenges to invigorate that role, and make it resonate with their personal strengths.

Moreover, achieving change is not merely a matter of "goal setting," which is an activity that is perhaps not always understood in the self-development and coaching world. You can't goal-set your way out of an emotional rut because the process of setting and pursuing goals, as conventionally practiced, is inherently crippled by a myopic oversight; these methodologies emphasize articulating goals but rarely ask you to interrogate *why* you're chasing them in the first place. That is the gaping hole at the center of many "self-improvement" regimens: they don't really examine what the individual holds dear, what he values, or what makes him tick. It is vital to have structure, but it has to be full circle— not linear.

THE GAME PLAN SYSTEM

The answer to this conundrum is the powerful life transformation system I've developed from coaching hundreds of clients (as well as much trial and error in my own life). It's called the Game Plan System, or GPS for short. The acronym is no accident, as the GPS symbolizes an existential navigational tool.

If you don't have a fixed destination, you're merely driving in circles, wasting gas, and squandering time; the longer you stay on the road purposelessly, the more likely it is your trip will end in a highway collision or roadside breakdown. Call it "itinerant inertia," a rather paradoxical phenomenon if you think about it—being constantly in motion, while at the same time, feeling that you're going nowhere.

It's a widespread, perhaps universal problem, and it afflicts highly accomplished people, as well. It means doing the same thing, and always moving, but never really knowing where you are going, or why. It might look fine from the outside (maybe you have a nice car), but you are the driver, and you need a meaningful trip and a true destination. This must be overcome if one is to get the most from life.

The GPS, therefore, is an apt metaphor: a navigational tool that helps you choose an objective and maps out the route to get there (circumventing roadblocks and handling detours that crop up along the way). In Chapter 2, I'll explain the GPS in depth. Throughout the book, I'll detail how you can build a GPS that allows you to discover and find the means of pursuing genuine purpose in your career and in your life.

IT'S NOT ABOUT "SUCCESS"

One factor that distracted me from discovering what really *drove* me was that I performed well in almost every job I had, even as I moved from industry to industry. I was committed to my work, but still felt a persistent and perplexing disconnect between career success and personal satisfaction. And after years of coaching, I've learned that my story is not at all uncommon. Many people will stay in a job because they are, by all standards, "good at it"—whether or not they are happy in their role or company. If a person is not gratified with his work, at least in some kind of meaningful way, he will feel it. This dissatisfaction will bleed into other areas of his life, and he will feel drained, and out of balance. With all of the time and energy we put into our careers, it should be something that benefits your life, not adds a burden to it. Ideally, our work should align with our talents, interests, and values. It is how we express ourselves, and a way we create and interact with the world.

In 2020, Gallup released the results of their Q^{12} Meta Analysis 20-year employee engagement study.

According to their research 58% of the workforce (they studied over 2.7 million workers worldwide) are "unengaged," and another 13% is "actively disengaged." These employees put time, but not energy or passion, into their work. To be "engaged" means a person is motivated in her job because she sees value in her efforts, is recognized for them, and has opportunities for growth. Engagement signifies a worker is committed to what she does. Most of us have seen an "actively disengaged" co-worker who leaves early, complains (or maybe rarely speaks), perhaps talks about greener pastures elsewhere, and does the absolute minimum required to get a paycheck. This person may not be very reliable, and will quickly leave her company for a slightly better offer.[2] They may perform their job competently, but as my coach Peter shared with me when I started working with him: *just because you are good at something, doesn't mean you should do it.*

Take Darren, one of my earlier coaching clients, who has also remained a good friend. At the time we met, Darren was a portfolio manager at a hedge fund– a type of money management firm that employs higher-risk

---

[2] Harter, Jim. (2020). Historic drop in employee engagement follows record rise. Gallup.com (2 July). https://www.gallup.com/workplace/313313/historic-drop-employee-engagement-follows-record-rise.aspx.

methods in the hopes of realizing large capital gains. Darren's charter was to get the highest return on the money he managed. As an expert short seller, that often meant betting against a company's success.

On the first day of coaching, he confessed he was sick and tired of shorting Chipotle stock—waiting for a bad quarter or a salmonella outbreak so he could get out of the position at the right time to make money for the fund. That can be a very negative worldview, setting up to strike when others find failure.

We worked through specific exercises and identified what would be meaningful for him. Darren was drawn, in the end, toward working in nonprofit or some sort of service. He wanted the opportunity to do some good. Contribute more, in his eyes. Others would indeed see "good" in betting against an organization—sending a message to an organization that they need to do better. It is one of the tools of accountability. It's not my, or anybody's, role to tell somebody what their definition of "good" is. Rather, it is to foster a discussion—and a partnership—to help them realize what it is for them. For Darren, he identified what would generate more energy and provide more meaning to his day-to-day.

Darren is now a curator for an internationally renowned speaking organization, where he finds innovative and inspiring speakers and puts together the slate for conferences. He gets to spend his time finding guests who can both entertain and enlighten, and then help these speakers prepare the best talk they can possibly deliver.

He had the courage to take a jump, and now he's excited about what he does every day. His daily life is in alignment with his desire to express himself, and he's much happier for it. It was a deliberate and intentional move, informed by conversations and exploration.

What Darren, many other clients, and I, myself, could tell you is that one of the reasons people can be hesitant to examine their lives is that they are worried about what they will learn. There is the risk that you would look at your life and suddenly realize you are on the wrong path completely. Are you going to need to make drastic changes?

These are emotionally charged questions and considerations, and they constitute one of the major impediments that your GPS must navigate around. I've created a step-by-step process where I can help people identify the right questions to ask and what to do with the answers we find. I work through them with clients and it helps them crystalize their ideas about where they are as well as where they want to be. Where they are today and where they want to be tomorrow.

First, I like to dispense with the ideas of life's purpose and your true passion and calling at this stage. The terms themselves, purpose and passion, can be overwhelming; we've assigned a heavy load of cultural baggage to these words. They are incredibly important and valid topics—and are useful—but the expectations that these concepts carry can be paralytic in nature. We often feel intimidated to think that we must unravel our specific life's greatest mystery, when approached with life purpose and passion, and the actual words get in the way of us moving forward. There is indeed a place for them, just not at the start. Instead, let's simplify. Starting from a place of lightness, ask yourself: What do you like to do? What do you need to do? How do you want to spend your time? What are the sorts of results you'd like to see? What impact do you want to have? What do you truly enjoy?

Starting with that line of inquiry tends to leave people excited and energized. They aren't scared of the big, unmanageable questions because we're working with small and manageable steps. They are lit up with the possibilities. They're curiously beginning to see the ways they can develop a life that works for them and that resonates with their innermost values and desires. I observe what happens to my clients as they open to the possibilities with this kind of inquiry. I follow their energy for clues. I listen not only to the words people say, but also how they say them. As a coach, I look for and follow energy. It's the truest indication, signal, of what my clients really want, even if they don't *yet* have the language to articulate it. Energy may hide. But it doesn't lie.

Do they look me in the eye when speaking? How does their body language change? What about the tone of their voice, their facial expressions, and speed of speaking? As we discuss various topics, they may sit up straighter, relax the furrows in their brow, and maybe even smile slightly. Generally, when I tell my clients what I've seen on this energy trail, they're responsive, intrigued, and inspired toward further exploration. It's a very natural progression, asking questions and observing a client's intuitive answers. Energy is how we express ourselves on the most fundamental and honest levels. What lights you up?

There is one thing that is vital to understand: the change (or changes) you need and want might not be a giant one. Drastic overhaul is not for everybody. You may not need to completely jump industries or change companies—or even roles—to find the sort of transformation that will reinvigorate your existence. Thousands of coaching sessions say drastic change is often not required.

In traditional coaching, the task involves identifying where someone isn't excelling, and finding a way to fix it. But I've found that approach is not a one-size-fits-all. My philosophy of coaching is strongly informed by Positive Psychology. I am not going to focus on what's wrong or "broken." Positive Psychology looks at what makes people happy, and how to truly enhance quality of life. I've seen that when we play to our strengths, we're not only gratified and more fulfilled, we also accomplish more. We're more successful, and we feel better about it. The key is confidence. When we can tap more into ourselves, it feels natural and effortless. It feels good.

Coaching from this positive angle, my clients and I focus on where they excel and what causes them to feel animated and alive. We then ascertain the concrete changes they can make to help draw more of those positives into their lives. I also use a variety of tools to identify their strengths, innate preferences, and predilections—and we put those to work.

There's a reason I named my coaching company Inflection Point. It's a term from mathematics that shows a single point on an XY-axis where a slope changes direction. The formula of an inflection shows where a line will go, and how its course will change.

Metaphorically, an inflection point is a decisive, catalytic moment that alters the trajectory of a person as an individual, or a business as a whole. That inflection point can be a dramatic one that sends you in nearly the opposite direction from where you were going before. But it can also be a subtle correction, a minor recalibration that brings you more in line with the way you should really be living. We experience inflection points more often than we realize. Probably, at this very moment, you find yourself at an important crossroads from which you can proceed in several directions, each of which could lead to radically different outcomes.

Whether the change is macro or micro, the most important thing is taking that first step toward finding your contribution to the world. This is the path that gives your life meaning.

Your path may be running a Fortune 500 company. It may be going on your own as an entrepreneur and disrupting an entire industry. It could be teaching the fourth grade. It could be performing as a cello virtuoso. It could be to thrive in your current role or excel in one to which you were just promoted. Everyone's answer is going to be a little different. That's the way it should be. The important part is finding what will help you embrace your strengths and develop a position that will allow you to put those assets into play, and make way for your success.

I am passionate about energizing other people's lives. I love being there as clients meet their true selves, and feel their souls stir. This newfound momentum empowers them to use that knowledge as a catalyst to build a rich and satisfying life free of nagging self-doubt and dissatisfaction. My joy is seeing individuals step into their own renaissance, powered by the energy they find within themselves.

It took me decades to recognize the difference between what I *should* do and what I *wanted* to do (what really...); moving from clue to clue, I learned how to organize my life in such a way that I could pursue my interests and passions, completely unfettered. I've synthesized my own lessons to create a simple and practical, yet powerful, system that anyone can tailor to his or her own needs. This book will save you years of wandering and misplaced effort. It may also prevent a fair share of pain. Know that it really is possible to live the life you've always imagined, one based on the activities and values that enthuse and engage you. Otherwise, you're just circling the vast cosmic highway, with no idea where you are and no clue as to where you'll end up.

Preserving Your Culture as You Grow

Every business that seeks to move into new markets, add team members, open new stores, or expand their horizons in any manner runs into the same challenge: How do you preserve your unique culture as you grow? The founders and the original team members have a strong sense of what their business is and what it stands for. But as more and more new hires come on board, and as you expand to additional locations, perhaps in states or even continents far from home, newer employees may simply see your company as offering not a mission but a job.

You could call it the "last mile" challenge. How do you deliver the same level of care for new customers or clients, when the people who are actually in contact with those customers are new to the company? They may have never even met the founder or have a clear sense of what the company's culture is meant to be. How can they represent your values to the buyer?

This was the dilemma facing a Paris-based fine jewelry company. Its founder and CEO wanted to work on two issues in our coaching sessions. First, the company was poised for expansion throughout Europe and even planning a flagship store in New York. How could they preserve the culture that had made the company so successful? The founder and his wife had been the main drivers of the company's success. How do you keep that same feeling of a family business when your ambitions point toward global expansion?

In addition, the couple wanted to fulfill a long-time dream of theirs: relocate from Paris, where the main shop and most of the employees were located, to Switzerland. How do you make a shift like that without upending everything you've built?

We began by looking for the adjectives that best described what made the company's culture so special. Those carefully chosen adjectives summarized, in a few pithy phrases, the culture of the company. The founder could now evangelize using those terms and explain to new team members just what the company stood for in language they understood. As the firm added new people, the executive leadership team was also using those same key words, over and over, as a way of explaining, "This is who we are. This is what we are working toward. This is how we go about our business to get there. And this is how we play together in the sandbox."

Before long, the new language became part of the interview process. Even before people were hired, they were exposed to the terminology that explained what made the culture of the company unique. As a result, the jewelry company was able to maintain its culture even as it expanded throughout Europe and beyond.

And as for the move to Switzerland? They no longer had to be afraid of it. As part of my client's Game Plan System, in the visualization step of the ACHIEVE model, he added a photograph of a particular home in Switzerland that he thought would be wonderful for him and his wife. A year later, they both moved into that very home, confident that the business would not suffer. As I always say, the power of visualization is not the sole possession of athletes or even businessmen! After all, seeing is believing—in the professional and personal spheres!

2

THE POWER OF GPS (THE *GAME PLAN SYSTEM*)

A typical NFL game lasts around three hours, from kickoff to when the fourth quarter clock ticks down to zero. The official game time is 60 minutes. And the actual duration of on-the-field action when the ball is in play amounts to 11 minutes.

By any of these metrics, a football game is an afternoon jaunt—over and done with in the time it takes to drive from Philly to New York, or half a sitcom's worth of actual gameplay action. But an immeasurable quantity of planning, practice, and preparation goes into each game. A battalion of coaches, assistants, analysts, physical therapists, groundskeepers, and other professionals spend Monday through Sunday prepping the strategy and conditions for the week's matchup.

As spectators, we get caught up in the moment-to-moment excitement, but we know that a football game requires careful administration. NFL coaches carry colorful laminated cards as they direct plays from the sidelines. These cards display 25 or more plays and game-specific considerations, so players will always have a plan to set into motion. These plays are written and drilled during team practices. The physical nature of the sport may look like brute chaos, but the mentality of football is to organize, through teamwork, toward victory. It reminds us of the old saying, "If you fail to plan, you plan to fail." You don't see NFL players going out on the field to "wing it."

Our daily lives, like a football game, require discipline and a plan. Things can be fast, brutal, and confusing, and with mounting pressure. If you leave the house without a plan, you're more likely to end up pummeled to the ground. We simply do not know what will really happen one day to the next or how hard the metaphorical game might be. If you want to take charge and become your own champion, you'd better learn to prepare.

THE INNER WORKINGS OF THE GAME PLAN SYSTEM

Sports provide meaningful philosophical reflections on human existence, but there is one key way in which the analogy is limited. Life is infinitely more complex than sports, especially when you talk about dreams and desires. The goal of a football game (and its outcome) is measured in strictly binary terms: you win or you lose.

Our discussion here is more nuanced and more complex. Sure, we all want to "win" at life, but the contours of winning and losing are vague and largely insubstantial. Furthermore, victory is not either/or. It is personal, situational, and dynamic. A fulfilled life does not concentrate on winning or losing, and it does not ask us to compete with others. I'd say it is a challenge, but not a competition. We must challenge ourselves to grow and to use our natural talents to their fullest expression. The more we flex our muscles, the more we learn. We participate in our own lives by deliberately creating them: knowing what we want, and making our plans come true. I believe a life well-lived is one where we challenge ourselves to enjoy it as much as possible (an enjoyment that is active, not passive). The challenge is to be honest. The challenge is not to settle for "good enough." The challenge is to discover our energies and do the work required to follow them forward. To find those energies, we must make a map.

That's the key distinction between the Game Plan System (GPS) and other coaching models. It's not oriented around an achievement-based outlook that focuses on setting objectives and pursuing (and achieving) them. Rather, it looks at life through a lens of Positive Psychology, the branch of psychological study that examines happiness and well-being, which are the ultimate priorities in any kind of decision-making. The GPS starts with examining what drives you, what is meaningful to you, what your values are, and which outcomes are going to be most reflective of who you are and what you need.

My clients are high-performing individuals, many of them luminaries in their fields. They are the big names and leaders of companies you would recognize. And as top performers, they're very good at defining their *what*—what they want to do or achieve—and their *how* (the plan of how to get it).

But finding their *why* is not as straightforward, and that's where things can get muddled. Consider if you aspire to land a managerial position with a top media company. Much of my coaching practice revolves around helping you explore the motivation behind that desire. I don't ask questions as a way to plump your ego, or simply make you feel good. That's not enough. Do I want you to see how that job/activity/degree will be stimulating intellectually? That's better, but it's still not adequate.

The *why* behind the goal has to resonate with something deep inside you, a fundamental part of who you are—or who you strive to become.

I spend a lot of time with my clients just getting at what is going to represent or manifest who they are intrinsically. It is not merely what you should do, but what you *could* do if you made decisions based only on your innermost, heart-and-soul-level desires.

What emerges from within? The point is for your outer actions to be congruent with your inner self. Do your behaviors, your words, your work, and your time commitments align with who you truly are? If that's lacking, there will be a kind of disconnect that will always nag you and make you feel uncomfortable no matter what gilded title happens to grace your office door.

This may seem to be abstract, touchy-feely stuff, but the magic happens when we winnow down our mix of passions, desires, wishes, images, impulses, and hopes into a simple, physical document—your personalized Game Plan System. Your GPS will help you prioritize and make decisions, and it will give you the boundaries and motivations you need, emotionally and intellectually, to keep your steps moving. The key is that *we write these things down*. Not unlike an NFL coach's laminated Game Plan card, your GPS is a concise yet detailed single page (front and sometimes back) you can place on your desk or pin on your wall. In this way, it provides a constant visual reminder that keeps you on track (it's laminated, too). It would be easy enough to devise a life plan and consign it to some digital file, or keep it on the back burner of your busy mind (where it has to share space with a million other things). But our goal is action, serious and real action. You need to see your plan to believe it. Figure 2.1 shows what a Game Plan System looks like.

One of the strengths of the GPS is that it's intended to be shared with associates, colleagues, friends and family, mentors, partners, and other stakeholders in your life's mission. One of the best practices for staying on track with a life or career plan is accountability,

[Initials] Game Plan

Month/Year

	[3-Word Summary #1]	[3-Word Summary #2]	[3-Word Summary #3]	[3-Word Summary #4]
GOAL	*I will...* [What do you want to achieve?]	*I will...* [What do you want to achieve?]	*I will...* [What do you want to achieve?]	*I will...* [What do you want to achieve?]
VISION	[Insert an image here: What does your goal look like?]	[Insert an image here: What does your goal look like?]	[Insert an image here: What does your goal look like?]	[Insert an image here: What does your goal look like?]
END	*By...* [When do you want to achieve this by?]	*By...* [When do you want to achieve this by?]	*By...* [When do you want to achieve this by?]	*By...* [When do you want to achieve this by?]
CONSEQUENCE	*So that...* [What does this mean to you?]	*So that...* [What might this mean to you?]	*So that...* [What might this mean to you?]	*So that...* [What might this mean to you?]
ACTIONS	*I will achieve this by...* □ [What action will you take to achieve this goal?] □ [Write "high-level" actions here and expand on these plans in the following slides.]	*I will achieve this by...* □ [What action will you take to achieve this goal?] □ [Write "high-level" actions here and expand on these plans in the following slides.]	*I will achieve this by...* □ [What action will you take to achieve this goal?] □ [Write "high-level" actions here and expand on these plans in the following slides.]	*I will achieve this by...* □ [What action will you take to achieve this goal?] □ [Write "high-level" actions here and expand on these plans in the following slides.]

Game Plan System™

Figure 2.1   A Sample Game Plan.

transparency, and alignment, which is only achieved by drawing others into your plan. Also, it's wonderful to have support, and a resourceful system to communicate with—for your sake.

One of the most famous examples of formulating a Game Plan was America's mission to the Moon, which captivated the nation and the world's attention throughout the 1960s. In 1962 President Kennedy announced, "We choose to go to the Moon in this decade and do the other things, not because they are easy, but because they are hard, because that goal will serve to organize and measure the best of our energies and skills, because that challenge is one that we are willing to accept, one we are unwilling to postpone, and one which we intend to win, and the others, too."[1]

That audacious statement kicked into gear an all-hands-on-deck process involving thousands of professionals in the space program (and many more stakeholders not directly involved but whose assistance was essential). It invigorated NASA, and America as a whole, with a clear and compelling sense of purpose and direction. And seven years later, the American flag was planted on the craggy gray expanse of the lunar surface.

---

[1] Kennedy, President John F. (1962). Speech at Houston Space Center (12 September).

The Moon mission was a tremendous mission of unthinkable scale, but it's analogous to how I go about creating goals with my clients. It starts by informing what goes on the Game Plan. Then we co-create the Game Plan, and the balance of the engagement is working the Game Plan, going on the journey together, and executing against it, as you'll discover throughout this book. After all, a goal is the outcome of how you organize your time, energies, and resources.

TRADITIONAL GOAL-SETTING VERSUS GPS: WHY SMART NEEDS TO BE SMARTER

One of the great lies (and there are many) of the self-development/personal development/coaching world is that all you need to effect a transformation in your life is to set the right goals and follow a process for achieving them (made possible by discipline). Not only does this miss the mark, but it can be dangerous, too. It causes a lot of angst and wasted time for the countless people who go down this road. The purpose of setting ambitions is to grow and learn as you meet them, not to be held in a feedback loop of want without follow-through.

Many people are familiar with SMART as a goal-setting program, a concept born from a paper written by businessman George T. Doran in 1981. He wrote "There's a S.M.A.R.T. Way to Write Management's

Goals and Objectives" as a curriculum for managers, so the model has a corporate perspective by nature. Doran emphasized the creation of goals that are Specific, Measurable, Achievable, Realistic, and Timely (there is some variation in the words in the acronym, but that's the gist). This method is not in and of itself wrong, per se. The problem is that SMART, and other conventional goal-setting systems, fall short of what is required. They are shallow. For one thing, it was meant specifically for business application, and it is intellectual, as opposed to comprehensive. Second, the system is limiting. It's not enough to have good intentions—one must know and feel the *why*, the underlying drivers of the goal.

What are the motivations and innermost intentions that produce your goals?

My own goal-setting system is ACHIEVE: each goal must satisfy seven criteria (see Figure 2.2). One of those is that it must be *consequential*—to embody something of great significance to me. That is what powers my progress toward the goal's realization. Knowing why something is important to you will drive you toward it versus just thinking that you'd like to have it.

If you've been beating yourself up for most of your adult life because you fail to follow through on the goals you set, or (just as common) you spend years chasing a goal only to discover that it wasn't really

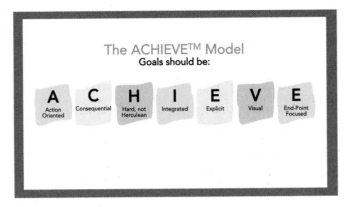

Figure 2.2   The ACHIEVE Model™.

what you wanted at all—you're not alone. For years I struggled in my own way with the ineffectiveness of the SMART system and other similar models. Many individuals work hard with the SMART model, but fall short. I, too, thought the formula was good enough, but I always sensed there was something vacuous about goal-setting on the whole. It wasn't until I began coaching that I realized the problem isn't with us—it's with the system.

Finally understanding that goal-setting doesn't work for most people was shocking but also tremendously liberating for me. I see the same shock and awe with many people I've helped see the light. If you've been slogging through your life chasing after something that no longer excites you (if it ever did), this is your way out of that trap (it's a trap you set for yourself, over and over again). It can even be argued that if you've wondered why checking all the boxes next to S-M-A-R-T has left you unfulfilled, then rest assured that the problem is not you. Working with your goals should be energizing. Challenging, yes. Not draining.

It's important to recognize that traditional goal-setting doesn't emphasize visualization, which constitutes a sizeable part of the GPS process. What will it look like when you achieve X? Is there flexibility in what it looks like? For example, if someone wants to run a marathon, do they visualize success as crossing a finish line? As just participating? As being one of the first to finish the race?

Once upon a time, I was fortunate to play on Columbia University's baseball team; I was good enough to have a shot at continuing to play after college before I decided to pursue other avenues. As an athlete, I learned the value of positive visualization—vividly imagining a successful action to make it more real, and priming my mind and body for achieving it.

It works, and the technique—which is used widely by athletes in all sports—is applicable in virtually any endeavor. Perhaps you've tried it, too. But I'm willing to bet you haven't really applied it to the big-picture process of figuring out what you really *want,* and reorganizing your life around that. Projecting an image in your mind of a desire is powerful; it nearly has a gravitational pull, dragging you from the realm of imagination into physical action, where your dreams actually do take shape.

THE "HEAD" COACH

The sad truth about traditional goal-setting approaches is that they just don't work. Most people don't get results. And even if they do, the results aren't meaningful because they didn't really think about why they wanted them in the first place. In truth, the system of traditional goal-setting can set us up to fail easily.

No one wants to admit this fact because there is such a strong social commitment in the current "self-improvement" system. We are told that goals are good, and that we should make them—even if we do not know why, or how. People have sunk a ton of time and intellectual/emotional labor into the goal-chasing process. There is now quite an industrial complex surrounding goals and discipline, and many individuals profit from the frustration of this process. Think of all the teachers, therapists, authors, guidance counselors, coaches, and speakers who want to talk to you about your goals.

The Game Plan System, in contrast, adds layers of intentionality, emotion, accountability, and principle to our planning practice. This allows us to make decisions and take actions with conviction, because we know that they are working in service of something of great importance to us. If we don't know what we're working on and what we're working toward, it's really hard to figure out what to do on a day-to-day, week-to-week, and month-to-month basis. I get fired up about this because goal-setting and other fallacies of conventional coaching just trap people further in the cycle of quiet desperation, and they end up walking in circles blindly, waiting passively for something to change. The GPS is the way out—and it starts today.

You can think of me as your coach, or guide. I am here to support and prompt the process of self-discovery and self-empowerment as you make it. Not in the way a therapist might (and we'll get into the distinction between therapy and coaching later), but in the sense that all external problems have an internal origin and an internal solution. The starting point for great transformation, whether professional, spiritual, emotional, or physical, lies within your very own mind.

My role, as your guide, is to reflect who you are and what you are doing. All the agency lies with you, the individual. I am here to listen and to inspire your path of self-discovery and self-empowerment.

You may be wondering what qualifies me to create GPS systems for my clients. There are many parts to the answer. I'll tell you a little about myself in the next chapter.

What you get by achieving your goals is not as important as what you become by achieving your goals.

— *Michelangelo Buonarroti*

From the Hockey Arena to the Business Arena

They say that if you do what you love, you'll never work a day in your life. Ted Page fits that description perfectly. He excelled in hockey in college and went on to enjoy an outstanding 10-year career playing professional hockey, including a stint as leader of the player's union. Ted was in his early 30s, and he had never held an office job. So here was the challenge: How does Ted, or any athlete, or anyone, for that matter, begin to contemplate a massive shift in career and identity?

Ted and I worked through the What, Why, How? model and we began to consider what he enjoyed, what lit him up, what energized him (the Sources/Drains exercise), and what he found most interesting. We then took his answers and examined what someone in his position, with that mindset, could manifest next in his life. Ted began to identify the different functions he would be interested in performing in the business world. Venture capital topped the list. Ted decided to get an internship at a venture capital firm. But another thing Ted had never done was go on a job interview!

Part of our work became interview prep. We talked about what kind of questions interviewers would ask. We developed the kind of answers that translated what he had learned on the ice into what he could do in the business world. Ted identified a series of skills relevant not just in the hockey arena, but also in the business arena. These skills included persistence, grit, bouncing back from injury, performing under pressure, teamwork, and not pointing fingers when things don't work out.

Ted secured an internship in venture capital and now he has a highly coveted general management training job at a consumer packaged goods company. Just because he was transitioning from hockey didn't mean he had to put his career aspirations on ice!

3

A LONG AND
WINDING ROAD

You want something more. And I understand the struggle behind finding your niche, your purpose, your passion, and your place in the world, whether it's a career that energizes you, or an activity outside of work you feel driven to pursue. My own journey has been professionally itinerant, as I moved from sports to finance to tech to media and entertainment, before finally arriving at my summit: being a coach.

In each position, and with each step, I have looked to what I might be excited about, letting passion guide the way. I understood that there was something else I wanted—and needed—to do. There was still a different kind of impact I wanted to have. I felt very aware of my unrealized potential, though I wasn't always sure what it was.

During this period of awareness and examination, one constant was the nagging feeling that even as I succeeded in my current position, something was missing. Now, I don't regret any of those experiences. There was no time lost. Each stride was tremendously helpful in broadening my professional skills and deepening my familiarity with different kinds of people and environments. In truth, I needed to do all of those things before I could figure out what I truly love—coaching and engaging audiences for a living. As many of my clients can attest, sometimes you have to do a lot of research. You need to ask a lot of questions, and feel your way toward the answers.

Having worked in so many settings—large companies, small companies, in the depth of recession, in the height of an economic boom, working under wonderful bosses and difficult ones, hiring people, firing people, succeeding and failing and succeeding again—has made me a more grounded, more empathetic person.

AN UNUSUAL UPBRINGING

Take a look at my adult life on paper, and you might make certain assumptions about my lineage and upbringing. Clean-cut business man from a well-connected, well-to-do family…. But I grew up with a blue collar ethos, in a family impacted by divorce, as well as periodic financial insecurity.

In the summer of 1982, when I was 10 years old, my parents split up and I lived with my father until I went off to college. Divorce was not so common in those days, and there is no easy way to reassemble a family structure. It was decided that I would live with my dad, and have visits with my mom. She and I are incredibly close today, and our relationship forms the foundation of my day-to-day life. Yet, the space between my parents put a lot of weight on me at a very early age. My older brother moved out about a year after my parents' divorce, so it was just me and my dad. I hadn't even entered the sixth grade yet, and I suddenly found myself very much on my own.

Like many single parents, my dad worked a lot (money was tight in those days), and I spent a lot of my time by myself. This was likely the formative period when I cultivated the self-discipline that is still one of my defining traits. That spirit of putting my head down and working hard kept me on track. No one had to tell me to do my laundry or complete my homework. That was good because, often, there was no one around to do these things for me. In many ways, I had to grow up fast. The independence ignited the flame within me. The motivation needed to come from inside. Much of my work today and the partnerships I foster seek to find the fire that burns within my clients.

This unusual upbringing left me with certain qualities that have shaped me. One is the ability to recognize—and seize—opportunities, and to make the most of scarcity. When I'm coaching someone, I help them embrace opportunities of their own, making the most of whatever situation they're in, good or bad. Not so many of my clients are in crisis. Some, in fact, do quite well and just need a coach to help maintain what they have worked so hard to accomplish.

Another quality that emerged in adolescence and defines me today is a strong-willed independence. Many of us have inhibitions that can keep us from adventuring and exploring. Since I have had to form my own structures and limits throughout my life,

I trust my own judgment. This gives me the freedom to venture out and try something new.

As I was free to pursue my own path, my independence helped give rise to an overwhelming desire to succeed. The choice was mine: I could fail in school or I could succeed, so I made a conscious decision to excel in the classroom. As a result, I graduated with honors managing the rigors of a student-athlete's life. I played football and baseball in the fall, basketball in winter, and baseball again in the spring.

Baseball was where I really stood out. By junior year I was named to the All-League and All-County team. A fractured vertebra, followed by seven months of rehab, set me back in my senior year, when I didn't play at all. This threatened to derail my athletic career just as it was blossoming, but I was still scouted by multiple colleges. In the end, I decided to go to Columbia University.

BRUSH YOURSELF OFF

Success often trumps failure in terms of visibility. You look at someone who's made it and your eye is drawn to the outward signs, material or otherwise, of their triumph. The years of hardscrabble effort and repeated failures sit invisibly in the background. Often, when we look at another person's accolades, we're seeing only the highlight reel—not the bloopers.

In my own life, I've had a failure for every victory. For instance, my college baseball career was nearly a wash.

In my first year at Columbia, I continued developing my skills, made the varsity travel team, and began to work off the rust of not playing for two years. And in my sophomore year, the coach named me the starting shortstop, making me one of the youngest starters on the team, and one of the youngest shortstops in the league. But I lacked confidence that I was worthy of the appointment and struggled incessantly with imposter syndrome. And when it came time to perform, I wasn't truly in the game; I was lost in my head.

The desire to excel in the role was so strong—and the attendant fear of failure so crushing—that I equated performance to be like the human need for love. Every mistake I made on the baseball diamond felt like someone close to you denying you the love you crave. It was punishing.

At the beginning of my sophomore season, we went to North Carolina and Florida to kick off our season; the pressure was so overwhelming that I started to sabotage myself. During the first 10 games, I played horribly, making mental errors in every single game. I watched most of the next 35 games of that 45-game season from the dugout. Coach had lost faith in me. Worse, I'd lost faith in myself.

The real turning point came after the end of that lack-luster sophomore year. During the season, I had hurt my shoulder badly (torn labrum) and had to undergo a pretty serious surgery given how much damage there was. I woke up from the anesthesia seized with panic, in incredible pain, and I was unable to move. It felt like I was never going to raise my arm again, never mind throw a ball. My whole athletic career, up in smoke. . .

And I asked myself, *Is this how you're going to go out?*

Grimacing through the post-op pain, I made a promise: *Hell no, this isn't the end. Not yet!* Even though baseball had caused me enormous stress, I knew that I'd regret it all my life if I gave up right there. I resolved to make a comeback. I loved the game.

So began the long, grueling process of rehab. As anyone who has been through major physical recovery can tell you, it's almost an athletic contest unto itself. You versus your own self-doubt: a test of wills, a battle of the spirit and the body allied together against physical trauma. Physical therapy is sometimes painful, sometimes boring, usually solitary (no cheering crowds to urge you on), and no one is going to congratulate you for doing it. I just had to grind through with the same independent resolve and quiet self-discipline that had served me so well when I was a kid, doing homework alone at the kitchen table. I believed in myself even when I did not feel well. I believed in myself even when I did not know where it would lead. This was the challenge I needed to grow and develop, not just as a baseball player, but as a young man. Through the rehab, and a commitment to working with a therapist to understand my thought processes, I began to better understand my why, as it related to baseball.

The following spring, I told Coach candidly that, though my last season had been something of a disaster, I had been working at rehabbing my shoulder and was determined to win back the starting role. In truth, I was overcoming the mental demons that had held me back.

I'll never forget his reply. It's one I've adopted as a regular coaching mantra. He said, "We'll see the performance on the field."

Coach's terse response was the correct one. Talk is cheap. We can make verbal commitments easily. Inspirational proclamations carry little weight without action. Lots of people set goals—what does it take to achieve them? Predictions and promises are cheap, but performance is what counts.

Ultimately, I worked hard to follow through. Coach could sense a change in me, so he put me in as starting shortstop again; not only was I hitting and fielding well, but I was able to rise above the mental issues that had plagued me the previous year. We won the division, and I was selected to the All-Ivy team. I had earned the respect of my teammates, even garnering some Most Valuable Player votes. And most importantly, I had begun to believe in myself.

In my senior year, I collected a few more honors, including some national awards. But winning MVP of the team was the most meaningful to me because I was selected by my teammates and coaches, the people who had seen me at my nadir, and recognized what I had done to bounce back.

I owed my turnaround to a few specific techniques, some of which have evolved into or inspired coaching practices I use with my clients (and in other areas of my life).

For example, if you ever played Little League baseball, I'm sure you remember getting yelled at by your coach or your dad to "get your head in the game, kid!" Despite what some may say, baseball is a fast-moving sport; there is, indeed, a pause in between pitches, but once the ball leaves the pitcher's hand, everything moves at a breakneck pace. A momentary distraction by any one player when the ball is in play can be devastating to the whole team.

During that comeback year, I knew that if I allowed myself to withdraw into my own head (with its constant, churning storm of self-doubt), it would take me out of the game and the same mistakes would repeat all over again. So on the baseball diamond, I wore a rubber band around my wrist, and every now and then I'd pull it back and snap it against my skin, just to remind myself: *Matt, you're here, be present, be focused, and concentrate on everything around you. Remember why you play. Enjoy the game.*

Every time distracting or self-disparaging thoughts invaded my mental space, a snap of the rubber band would chase them away. It stopped the ruminating thoughts. Most importantly, it helped me focus on my love for the game (why I was there, in the first place) rather than the performance pressure I pushed on myself. It only took a few games of doing this before I was mentally conditioned to feel the energy of what I was doing, and not fight it. Just the presence of the band on my wrist was enough.

In coaching, I help clients "get out of their heads" by channeling their hopes and anxieties into a space where they can be dealt with. We short-circuit ruminating thoughts. Usually that means putting them down on paper and attacking them, safely, there. Snapping their mental and emotional rubber bands, so to speak, brings them into reality—instead of swirling around in a storm of negative thoughts and feelings. To this day, you may still see me with a rubber band around my left wrist.

CONTROL THE CONTROLLABLES

You can't control what's outside of you. I couldn't control whether another better player was going to compete for the shortstop position. I couldn't control what my coach would ultimately decide. But I did have domain over my own performance.

I entered physical rehabilitation with a dogged determination to return to the field and win back my starting role, and in a deeper sense, to reclaim the excitement for the sport that drove me in the first place. I wasn't going to get psyched out by mistakes anymore. I wouldn't blow the whole game because I bobbled the ball or struck out at one at-bat.

Ideas like "control the controllables" and "performance on the field" don't just apply to college or pro level sports. I have coached Little League, and trained eight-year-olds in this discipline, too. You can be right where you need to be to catch a ground ball speeding toward you, but maybe it hits a rock and suddenly its trajectory changes. That doesn't matter—you can't control a moving ball. What matters, and that which you can control, is where you position yourself on the field, that you got a good night's sleep, that you and your teammates are working together and feeling like a team. How you react to the speeding ball, with whatever direction it takes, depends on your mindset and readiness. Both of these take shape long before you even step on the field. Attitude and preparation are aspects you can very much influence. Will you be able to catch that baseball if you are anxious or exhausted? You can't control the outputs, but you can almost always determine the inputs, or the controllables.

"Control the controllables" is applicable to anyone at any stage of life. A fifty-three-year-old broadcasting executive can't control what the network decides to do. He can't say what's going to happen after the next merger. But he can research markets, build and lead an excellent team, and propose innovative programming. He'll be a success if he follows through on the things he *can* do.

Fretting over things that are beyond our influence is a futile exercise that only amplifies our troubles. Self-actualization—the process of becoming your fully realized self, becoming the person you always wanted to be—is not solely about individual willpower and drive. It's also partly about acceptance and letting go. While something of a paradox, the less we focus on the outcome and instead channel the energy into what we control, the *more* likely we are to accomplish that desired outcome.

MORE THAN A PAYCHECK

For most athletes, college is the terminus of their sports career. Only a select few take a shot at pro ball, which in baseball means grinding years in the minor leagues as you try to claw your way up from the three levels of A-ball to AA to AAA to the majors—the dream of every kid tossing a ball around in his backyard.

For me, it would have been a long shot, but I was skilled enough to give it serious consideration, and at least take the first step. However, after college, I opted to enter the workforce instead, believing it offered a path more in line with what I felt drawn to do. I wanted to see what was out there, and what I could do.

And so, I parlayed my baseball experience and hard work in the classroom to land a job in the fixed income (bond market) trading division at a prominent investment bank in New York City. Mine was a highly coveted job, and there was plenty of competition. For a 22-year-old in his first job and who had never experienced the world of high finance, the dynamic trading-floor environment was exhilarating. Each day brought a fresh challenge to deal with and something new to learn, so the work was never monotonous, even if the hours were grueling. Fixed income sales and trading, and the trading floor specifically, has a cutthroat reputation, but at least in our department, the atmosphere was more collegial and collaborative. It was an excellent starting point for a recent college graduate.

I also gained fresh insight into human psychology, which would be a constant throughout all my successive, varied positions: each job deepened my understanding of people and what makes them tick. There was one trader, a guy named Charles, who was notorious around the trading floor for his short temper—the kind of guy who had a penchant for growling at people, especially the more junior folks like me. More than one keyboard met a grim fate when he threw them at the monitor in a fit of anger. People tended to avoid Charles, as did I—at least at first.

In time, however, I cultivated a meaningful relationship with him. He was gruff and volatile on the surface, but he had a lot to offer, and was willing to mentor select younger employees. You just had to know his personality. Once I figured out what frustrated him, I'd do the opposite. You had to understand his motivations and play into that. What he wanted and why he wanted it. What drove him. I discovered that while Charles was a tough nut to crack, he was a good guy to have a working relationship with. He ended up writing an encouraging end-of-year review for me. Given that he was a man disinclined to dishing out compliments, it made the review all the more meaningful.

Despite the perks of the job, and the fact I was making a name for myself, I knew a long-term commitment to the fixed income trading floor wasn't my place. As I mentioned in Chapter 1, I did well enough in the role that the company wanted to promote me to associate. But it wasn't a proper fit. I was there for a few years, but the prospect of making a lot of money was not enough to compensate for the fact that while I enjoyed the work, my heart was no longer in it. I also noticed a certain ennui—a malaise even—among some of my colleagues, including those who were pulling down seven figures a year. Beyond a certain point, the paycheck serves as an inadequate balm for feeling emotionally or spiritually out of place.

My time with the investment bank did help hone certain skills that are useful in coaching. For one thing, I learned how to work with and understand different kinds of driven, high-achievement people. Another was more methodological. The best traders develop a process, and stick to it. They set goals and tailor their process toward achieving those goals, which is something I apply in coaching, as well. The position also required the ability to synthesize data points from different sources, recognize patterns in that data, and make informed decisions. Human behavior can be studied in the same way—we are complex beasts, with many emotional threads, disparate impulses, different factors pulling us this way and that. But recognizing *patterns* in that constellation of beliefs, wishes, fears, dreams, etc., is essential to diagnosing a problem, or identifying a positive trend in a client's life.

I also noticed that the people in finance who really stood out in their performance *loved* the work. They devoured newspapers and trade magazines and dove into their Bloomberg terminals to learn as much as they could. What was interesting enough to me was invigorating to them. It was an early lesson that passion for the work you do makes all the difference.

BACK TO SCHOOL

I decided to leave my finance job and go to business school. Not the easiest decision given the desire for financial security that my upbringing had instilled in me. I was rejected by Harvard Business School the first time around, but I reapplied again with another year of maturity, and was accepted.

People thought I was nuts to leave the lucrative career track offered by my previous employer, especially since I was paying 100% for business school out of my own pocket.

Nevertheless, my instinct was proven correct. Attending graduate school was the best decision I could have made. I had an opportunity to learn from not just some of the most knowledgeable professors in the world, but also some of the smartest, most dedicated, and most inspirational classmates—one of whom became my wife a year after we graduated.

The business school curriculum emphasized case studies. The case studies served not just to provide practical insight about specific business scenarios as much as they taught us how to think like business owners. We were encouraged to diagnose, analyze, reason, and synthesize a solution by inserting ourselves into the specific situation and asking: What would I do? That methodical approach to problem-solving influences me today in how I work with clients. I've adapted the diagnostic, prognostic schema from the context of a business to the realm of the individual client.

One of the pillars of the Harvard Business School curriculum is a course called Leadership and Organizational Behavior, which first-year students are required to take. In one class, we were analyzing a case study in which the protagonist of the story had to choose between employment at one of two companies.

One student ventured that Company A was the obvious choice because the position paid more, was more prestigious, and offered a clearer avenue to professional success.

Almost reflexively, my hand shot up.

"Matt," the professor said. "Looks like you're jumping out of your seat."

"I don't think that's the best choice, actually," I said. "It really depends on what the definition of success is, whether this person should take that job or not."

"And how would you define success?" the professor countered.

"I think success results from having the desire and ability to listen to oneself and then the courage to act upon it," I replied.

It was an unexpected answer in a room full of people who were brilliant and, for the most part, expecting a more conventional notion of "success." But in saying those words, I felt the inkling of a deep-seated truth that was yearning to get out. At the time, the ideas that form the philosophical bedrock of my coaching practice were still emerging, but that was one of the earlier light bulb moments when I realized that there's a missing ingredient to the usual wisdom about life and career.

After business school, I went to work with several different companies, large and small. I had roles in sales, business development, marketing, and general management. I did well in each of those roles, but still found, time and again, that I wasn't quite doing what I wanted.

Ironically, success trapped me. During my time at MTV Networks, I regularly put up strong numbers in the large ad sales division. The title (and salary) were respectable, and I enjoyed the travel, but the work was unsatisfying. I struggled with myself to find the meaning in selling advertising solutions. These just weren't the sorts of things that were important to me. However, I got close with my clients and learned how to help solve their problems. I was really catering to the other person's wants and needs more than selling an actual product or service. Ad sales are generally a numbers game, but I saw it as an act of listening. I was hitting my sales targets and getting bonuses every year, but money was not my meaning.

It was becoming undeniably clear that *success alone is unfulfilling if you're succeeding in a role that doesn't excite you.* I refused to settle even if that meant lifting my tent stakes and moving on again, perhaps changing fields entirely. The prospect of a mid-career jump is always fraught with risk. But the real risk was in staying where I was. I wasn't happy. Every day stretched in front of the last, and none of them held what I needed to have the sort of life I felt was meant for me. The concept of unrealized potential frightened me the most. I had a few different jobs after my time at MTV Networks, and always had the same tenacious internal questions.

I was married by then, and I wanted my wife to get back the dynamic and passionate guy she married. I wanted my kids to see someone excited and engaged in his career and his life. I wanted to truly make a personal impact and change people's lives for the better.

I'd begun to engage a business coach of my own. One thing that coach said to me really crystalized the issue. He told me, "Matt, just because you're good at something, it doesn't mean you should do it."

Each time I made a move, I was able to identify the elements of what I wanted a little more clearly and move closer toward the work I'm doing today. I paid attention to how I felt and to what lit me up. This meant being extremely honest with myself. Even when the path wasn't clear, when the jigsaw puzzle didn't have as many pieces assembled as I would have liked, I tried to follow where the energy was taking me.

Regardless, the multitude of experiences and roles I had en route to coaching exposed me to a broad array of personalities, problems, challenges, and environments, which has made me better equipped to address my clients' needs. And through it all, I learned much more about myself. Of course, that journey of self-discovery never really ends and is continual. That very fact makes life both frustrating and exhilarating.

One of the ironies of my journey is that for years I was chasing satisfaction I believed would come from merely getting to the next higher rung on the so-called ladder. But each promotion, raise, award, or successful job interview failed to deliver more than a momentary spike of achievement. Sure, I had done something—but what did it mean?

I understand that I was half-right—there *is* a thrill in accomplishment. But for me, true accomplishment is the *vicarious* sort I experience when clients experience what they've been pursuing. Helping others, and being with them in their moments of triumph, is much more satisfying to me. We go on a journey together, share in the work and the joy. I seek the fist-pump expression of success my clients make when they are on their road and/or they have achieved something of meaning. That's my fuel. It's the ultimate expression of energy.

In the next chapter, I'll discuss how the what, why, and how interact to form your unique path.

4

WHAT/WHY/HOW?

One of the strengths of the GPS process is that it applies a methodical approach to large problems. Instead of diving into a maelstrom of possibilities, I work with my client to develop a concrete plan in which the what, the why, and the how (see Figure 4.1) are clearly defined: **What** do you want, **why** do you want it, and, **how** will you get there?

In other words, we want to go slow to go fast—"ready, aim, fire" instead of "ready, fire, aim" (or perhaps even more extreme "fire, ready, aim").

The process can be a little circular in a way. These what/why/how questions reinforce one another and build on each other. It's rarely linear. The important thing is that this sort of thinking starts to help you articulate your ideas and make them concrete. When

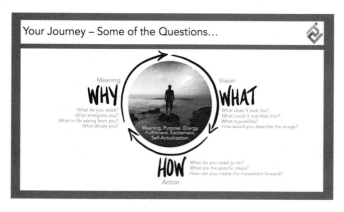

Figure 4.1 Your journey—What, Why, How?
Source: Ssokolov/Shutterstock.com

you have them down on paper, they're not big and amorphous and frightening anymore.

Emotionally charged topics can trigger ruminating thoughts. Your mind is trying to solve for something it doesn't have enough information for or it doesn't have the ability to process at that moment. This simple framework helps calm those swirling thoughts.

Let's take a fictional coaching client—call her Carol. She's in upper management at a major media company, but she's feeling somehow unfulfilled. I sit down with her and we talk, and with my questions and by listening carefully, I get to know her. I want to try to understand what drives her. I start to get a sense for who she is. I get her talking about her "why"—what values and activities really get her motivated. Maybe she really comes alive when she is looking at data and trying to find patterns that can help her predict where her industry is going next. So, what she wants out of life is more of those aha moments.

Or, it could be that we start with a "what." She may be looking for a position with more prestige and challenge than she has right now. We could even start by delving into a "how," and discuss the activities she feels merit her time and energy, and figure out a "what" that will make those part of her every day. Then, we discuss a strategy to get her there.

Though there is flexibility in this dialogue, it is important to emphasize that if a client wants to focus on the what or the how, we spend the requisite time understanding the why, what is driving the what, or driving the desire to act. This becomes foundational for the partnership.

Another client of mine (let's call her Victoria) works closely with a well-known celebrity chef. Recently, the chef founded a chain of restaurants that Victoria helps oversee, but he runs the business in something of a sloppy manner. He understands his why, but he's less clear on the what. Consequently, he—and everyone who works for him—is pulled in 10 different directions on any given day. Victoria compares him to a speedboat that's been lifted out of the water—there's so much kinetic energy pulsing through spinning propellers, but the boat isn't going anywhere. For Victoria, it's exhausting—mentally, physically, and emotionally.

The what, why, and how only work if they are in balance—with emphasis on the why. It really is like chemistry: combine any two ingredients without the third, or pour in too much of one, and the mix of substances remains inert. But when all three are in proportion, they react to one another in a powerful way that gives you the forward propulsion you need to get where you need to be.

THE WHY

The why is the starting point, because that's where the meaning and consequence lie, and without consequence (the "C" in ACHIEVE), everything falls flat.

The "what" is closely linked with the "why," but many people—including many coaches, psychologists, and other well-meaning advice givers—overemphasize the former at the expense of the latter, perhaps because the what is defined in more concrete terms (an activity or pursuit) while the why by nature is more conceptual and personal. However, *you cannot have one without the other.*

If your why isn't in sync with your what, you'll be like the aforementioned chef, drifting rudderless in the sea, carried whichever way the wind takes you. And if your what is divorced from your why, a vague existential malaise is likely to emerge in the gap between them. Over time, you'll be beset with the feeling that even as you put in effort, you don't know what fundamental purpose your effort is serving. You'll secretly wonder, "What is the point of all this?" And that nagging feeling can, over time, metastasize into the kind of quiet desperation that erodes a vibrant, purposeful life.

This is why, when I work with clients, we don't just analyze activities/realms/pursuits that interest them; we really try to dig deep and probe the *essence* of each thing, and what makes it meaningful to them. It's usually in that hidden layer where the "why" is discovered. It's a bit like utilizing the "five whys" process, a technique that helps get at the root cause of a phenomenon.

This can be exciting, eye-opening, and even life-changing for clients because they start to realize while they always knew they enjoyed X, they now realize they enjoy it for a completely different reason than they suspected. The converse is also true: you might resent the job you've been boxed into for 20 years, only to discover through the coaching process that it's not the job itself that frustrates you, but one or two specific components of it. And when you make that discovery, you can separate the good from the bad, the sources of energy from the drains.

Without a why, you're basically just going through the motions. And maybe you're very good at that! Perhaps you've done it so long that it's second nature—you are on autopilot. Autopilot isn't necessarily the worst thing. It works very well for airplanes! But it means your actions are all function and no form. Pure utility, but they lack heart and soul. They produce a life of quiet desperation.

The why is a slippery concept, hard for most of us to pin down because it touches on such deep, philosophical, existential notions as "What is my purpose on earth?" or "What imparts meaning to my life?"

I've developed a methodical process to demystify these questions and aid clients in unlocking their why. There are several techniques I employ, but one is a questionnaire that asks things like:

When have you felt most alive? What have been sources of energy for you? What has drained energy from you? When have you done something where you've lost all track of time? What are some things you've always desired to do but haven't?

The assessment tries to get at who you are, what you naturally gravitate toward, and what puts wind in your sails (see Figure 4.2).

One of the most effective exercises is what I call "sources and drains." First, you draw a line down the

What Energizes You? What Takes Energy Away?

Current/Former Job; Volunteer Positions/Non-Profit Board/Community Involvements.
(Be specific – focus on the tasks; environment; team/no team)

Energy Sources	Energy Drains

Figure 4.2   What energizes you/What drains your energy?

middle of the page. On the left, list activities that energize and excite you, that light you up—sources of energy. On the right, list activities that drain your energy or dim that inner light.

For instance, when I was in a business development/sales position at MTV Networks, I would have named "human capital" as a source—seeing other people develop and thrive and grow, and promoting the folks I work with and bolstering their opportunities. I didn't love all aspects of my job, but I was inspired by that one—it meant a lot to me. What strengths or skills does that imply? Creativity, social intelligence, love of learning, and curiosity.

The right side of that paper might have included "working in a corporate office," a common dislike among white-collar professionals. How can you tie together the "sources" while eliminating the "drains"? Finding a job or activity or setting where this is possible provides a space for self-discovery.

Another important part of the process is that, with the client's permission, I'll talk to their friends, family, spouse, and maybe even co-workers. People don't often see themselves clearly (whether they're too generous or too self-critical) and they overlook aspects of their personality that others pick up on. Soliciting the input of others ensures the assessment is comprehensive and well-rounded. Moreover, this loops other people into the client's process as *stakeholders*. They're not merely providing information to kick off the coaching; they're being recruited as active participants in my client's mission.

THE HOW

Of course, the "what" and the "why" are of little use without a "how" to achieve them. If the what and why are concepts, the how is execution. And execution is where the real work is done. If you've determined a "what" and a "why" that really resonate with and enliven you, the "how" should fall into place naturally. As Nietzsche wrote, "If we have our own why in life, we shall get along with almost any how."[1]

There are coaches who have PhDs in organizational psychology or social work or some other field, and many of them are very good coaches; however, their outlook tends to be quite different from mine. It is more conceptual rather than practical and action-based. They may spend a large amount of time with their clients on planning, musing, and analyzing. The coaching they provide is heavy on the what and why.

---

[1] Nietzsche, Friedrich. (1889). "Maxims and Arrows" from *Twilight of the Idols.*

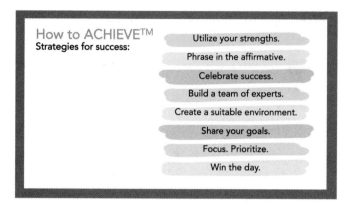

Figure 4.3   How to ACHIEVE™: Strategies for success.

Other coaches are more like career consultants; they will motivate you, fix your resume, and edit your cover letter, then help you with interview prep before sending you off on a round of interviews. These coaches are more action-oriented but they often lack a philosophical framework. They are big on the how.

My approach harmonizes introspection and action in the ideal proportions. I use the following eight-step process, visualized in Figure 4.3, to carry out the "how."

1. *Draw on your strengths.* This technique is heavily influenced by Dr. Martin Seligman's work in Positive Psychology. The idea is that if you put to use that which you are naturally drawn to or excel at, you are going to

be happier and more fulfilled, and will have a much greater chance of achieving your desired outcome. One assessment I use is the Values in Action Survey to pinpoint one's unique strengths.

2. *Phrase things in the affirmative.* This is a psychological trick that harnesses the power of linguistic nuance to encourage a more positive, can-do outlook. Instead of phrasing actions, goals, or ideas in the negative, you phrase them in the positive, and in doing so reframe them in a self-empowering manner. For example, if you say, "I don't want to wake up in the morning and feel exhausted," and enlist a coach to help you remedy that, you rephrase this problem as a solution: "I want to wake up feeling rested." This nudges the subconscious mind toward thinking about things in terms of not what you *don't* want to do, but what you *want* to do. Though it's subtle, it really does bolster your optimism and agency.

3. *Celebrate successes along the way.* This is especially important in long-term projects where the overall objective may not be achieved for a year, two years, or more. That's a very protracted timeline, and it's hard to sustain

enthusiasm for so long without some validation along the way.

We spend about two decades in our formative years attending school, where regular feedback, evaluation, and encouragement is a cornerstone of the education system. But as soon as we leave that world, the feedback drops off. In our professional as well as our personal lives, we're rarely praised for our accomplishments; in some jobs, you might not get any feedback until you screw something up, even if you do everything else right.

This is unfortunate, because adults, too, thrive on validation for small accomplishments. It's important to recognize and revel in the small milestones that lead up to the major achievement. These celebrations are like little bursts of nitrous oxide that propel your vehicle forward on a long and winding race.

At the end of each coaching session, the client and I celebrate its completion, and the progress made. No success is too small to recognize.

4. *Assemble your team of experts.* Few endeavors are achievable through individual will alone. You need coaches. You need assistants. You

need stakeholders. You need mentors. You need partners.

In short, you need a team. If you're the CEO of your life, think of these people like your "personal Board of Directors." They should include people of different strengths and backgrounds that complement each other (and you). They should be supportive, but fair and firm. You don't just want a bunch of "yes men"; you want people who are eager to see you succeed but will also deliver constructive criticism when it's needed.

When recruiting mentors for your personal board, remember that the best kind of mentor is someone who has been in your shoes and has achieved the very thing you're working to achieve now. Not only do they know how it's done, but they can empathize with the arduousness of the struggle. You also may truly need an expert: a public-speaking specialist, a nutritionist, etc., depending on the goal.

5. *Create a suitable environment.* Even the best farmer in the world can't grow an orchard in the desert. You need to cultivate an environment that is conducive to your pursuits. Environment in this context could mean the

immediate physical environment, and improving it might be as simple as moving some furniture around. For example, if your goal is to improve your sleep hygiene, maybe that necessitates removing the TV from the bedroom. Perhaps you need to establish a quiet zone in an otherwise noisy house. If you want to be a more present leader, open your door and walk the floor and interact with people.

We might also mean environment in the broader sense: if the company culture at work is killing your creativity and drive, you need to find ways to change it (or leave completely). Eliminate environmental factors that impede your ability to work toward your mission and build up those conditions that allow you to flourish.

6. *Share your goals.* The mere act of thinking about a goal boosts the odds of reaching it. If we think about it and write it down, the chance of success is increased further. If we think about it, write it down, and verbally share it with somebody, the odds are increased even more. And if we think about, write it down, verbally share it, and hand it off to somebody, it puts us in an even better position.

That's why every GPS I co-create with my clients is blown up and laminated—it's designed to be put on a wall, passed around, and shown to others who care about or have a stake in your success.

My wife and sons all have a copy of my own Game Plan. Consequently, I'm on the hook for following through. Not that my 16-year-old is checking in with me each week, like, "Dad! How's that plan coming together!?" But just knowing he has it in his hands (or, more likely, under a pile of laundry somewhere, but in his room, nevertheless) produces a certain psychological benefit to me. It keeps me accountable.

In 2015, psychology professor Gail Matthews led a study at Dominican University that found that more than 70% of participants who sent a weekly progress report to a friend reported successful goal achievement, compared to only 35% of participants who did not share their goals (and didn't write them down). The study emphasized the value of sharing goals for a variety of reasons: helping to clarify ambitions and better understand them, having support, building trust, being accountable, feeling not alone, making regular updates, and acknowledging your growth process. Communicating goals makes their achievement all the more meaningful. Of course, who you share with makes all the difference. Writing down your goal(s) and then saying them out loud, activates a physical-neurological-emotional drive to follow through.[2] Future research will hopefully shed more light on the effectiveness of this rule. But in my experience with hundreds of clients, sharing your goals produces a net benefit.

7. *Don't bite off more than you can chew.* Ambition is a type of hunger, and sometimes our appetite overwhelms our body's ability to take it all in. Less is more—the more goals and to-do items you pile on, the less likely you are to achieve all (or any) of them. It's dispiriting to check off 4 items from the list when there are 20 more stretching to the bottom of the notepad, a visual testament to all you haven't accomplished, when instead you should be

---

[2] Matthews, Gail. (2015.) Goals research study. https://www.dominican.edu/sites/default/files/2020-02/gailmatthews-harvard-goals-researchsummary.pdf.

encouraged by the things you have completed. It is better to do 4 things well with all your heart, rather than 20 things haphazardly, just to get them done.

Concentrate on the three or four most important things you have to get done and bring all your strength to bear on those items. *Then* you can move on to the next set of challenges. Don't overload your plate. We have only so many hours in the day so we need goals that are well-selected. Focusing on a few thoughtful challenges could have a dramatically positive impact across the entirety of somebody's life. Well-chosen goals have a cascading effect on many aspects of one's life. Let's put our attention and energy on things that really matter, leaving enough space for reality and the things we can't control. Maybe you wanted to check something off your list today, but the line was long at the DMV and your child came home from school with a fever. A well-lived life is an à la carte menu at a nice bistro, not an all-you-can-eat buffet.

8. *Win the day*. You've probably heard that the best way to achieve a major goal or master a long-term project is by breaking it into

smaller tasks. For an undertaking the time-line of which is measured in years (or is even indefinite), break it up temporally into smaller units, and focus on winning each day. It's like that favorite post-game press conference cliché of head coaches everywhere: "We're just going to take it one day at a time. . ."

If you've accomplished your three or four tasks for the day, then mark off "WTD" on your calendar or notepad or Excel file. At the end of the week, hopefully you have five or six Ws or even seven Ws lined up, a visual testament to your diligence, resilience, and progress. Repeat ad infinitum, and nothing can stop you.

It's a little like investing for retirement. If you put $100 a week in an IRA, each contribution doesn't seem like much. But if you do it faithfully for several decades, compounding interest will grow that money into a fortune. Working toward a long-term goal is simi-lar; your sustained effort, week over week, is banked in your personal vault and this effort will "bear interest" and compound until eventually developing into something much grander than a string of Ws on your calendar.

When the what and the why take shape, the how emerges naturally. And when the how is systematized using this eight-step process, the sometimes nebulous-seeming why and what are reified (made real). If you've never used these techniques before, it might seem daunting, like being handed a tool belt with eight different tools and being told, "Okay, go build yourself a house."

And what if you understand your *why* but don't know what is your *what*? I call this process of discovering your calling "finding your Piano Man." In the next chapter, I'll talk about what that means, and how you can find yours.

Going All In

We all know that social media promotes a ton of FOMO, or fear of missing out, among people in their teens and 20s (and perhaps older folks as well!). But there's a ton of FOMO in the business world, too. Every career choice has attendant opportunity costs—if you take job A, you may miss out on the excitement and success you could enjoy if you took job B. Some people aren't bothered by FOMO; they see an opportunity and run with it. But for others, fear of missing out on, say, the next hot tech IPO, can be absolutely paralyzing, and can keep them from making any decision.

Ultimately, one of the worst decisions you can make is not to make any decision at all. Other people and outside forces will plan your career for you, and they may not always have your best interests at heart. So how do you make a decision when there are at least two, and often more, compelling choices?

This was the dilemma facing Diane Goldman, a highly successful tech executive in Austin, Texas, with a highly respectable track record as a chief revenue officer. Diane had a choice. She could open up her own shop, and consult to a wide range of companies, which was where her heart was directing her. Or she could take a chief revenue officer position at a hot new tech firm.

If she followed her heart and opened up her own shop, the FOMO would be all but unbearable. What if that hot new tech company turned out to be the next hot tech IPO? How much money would Diane be leaving on the table if she were to go the consulting route and start her own business?

I asked Diane to put both feet into one opportunity—either opening her consultancy or taking a CRO position. She would not be successful simply pondering both options. Together, we considered a scenario in which she would give herself one year to focus on creating a consulting company, and to be "all in" doing just that. I suggested that she not entertain chief revenue officer roles during that year, no matter how enticing, and that she set aside her fears about becoming irrelevant and not getting calls for such positions because she was now a consultant.

Diane took my suggestion, dedicated herself wholeheartedly to her consulting practice, and building an organization around her individual efforts. Diane had her best year financially of her entire career. All because she made a choice, put a timeline on it, stuck to it, and avoided distractions.

Over the course of those 12 months when Diane was establishing her consulting firm, we spoke a lot about her future. She said that she wanted to create something self-sustaining where she could leave behind a legacy, perhaps something even greater than a company where she's employing many people. Now Diane is securing her legacy, and best of all, she doesn't feel as though she's missing out on anything.

5

WHAT'S YOUR PIANO MAN?

Very few people actually have a fully formed idea of what they *really* want, some central activity around which they base their life. When I explain this fact to clients, it often comes as a relief, as many of them feel like they're doing something wrong because they haven't discovered "their one true passion."

Society glorifies people who are single-mindedly dedicated to a single pursuit. Because they possess a sheer, raw enthusiasm for a specific activity, they are the ones who tend to rise to the top of their respective field; yet they have a disproportionate visibility in society that leads us to believe that this clarity of purpose is normative—a default human quality that, if you lack it, you're somehow inadequate, aimless, or indecisive.

No one should feel inadequate for not having found their single-minded passion. It's very common; in fact, based on my coaching experience, I'd say 80 to 90% of people still aren't sure of their niche. That doesn't mean they lack ambition or purpose. Rather, it just means that most people who want to accomplish great things are not sure of which great things they want to accomplish.

I used to experience a certain envy for those people with an inborn passion that leads them definitively onto a certain path in life—those who seem to "just know" what they want to do and they do it. I had a friend whose overriding ambition, since the age of eight, was to sing and dance on Broadway. That's a notoriously difficult career to follow, but at a young age this person knew what the mission was. There were no other options, that was the plan—and my friend has made a great living, and a great life, dancing on the Great White Way.

The most anxiety-inducing part of the long journey of self-actualization is not the hard, often decades-long work you have to do to get from Point A to Point B. The anxiety comes when you don't even have a clear idea of what Point B is, and that comes from not understanding yourself well enough—the *why*.

Nevertheless, there's also something to be said about *not* knowing. It's liberating to recognize you are not alone in wrestling with some ambiguity in your vision for your own life, and it's exhilarating to accept that if your path is not a linear one—there will be many false starts and dead ends and detours along the way—that just means you get to try out a lot of interesting things as you go.

Steve Jobs is a fine example of this kind of existential circuity. That may come as a surprise to some readers since Jobs is known for being a visionary with unparalleled drive and focus. Perhaps he was later in life. But it wasn't always that way.

Jobs didn't declare at age eight, "I want to found a technology company," and then drive relentlessly toward that goal. On the contrary, his path was nonlinear: he dropped out of college after one semester, hung out with his on-again, off-again girlfriend for a while, and audited a calligraphy course (which later influenced Apple's brand-defining aesthetics). Later, he worked as a technician for Atari, then went on a kind of "spirit quest" to India, came back, dropped acid, and lived on a commune. All this before he even attempted to start a business.

The point is that by living, wandering (literally and metaphorically), learning, and trying different things, bit by bit, Jobs' wild constellation of ideas, impulses, and interests came together to form a gestalt—a whole that is more than the sum of its parts—which eventually coalesced into the global company we know as Apple. The connecting principle was that he always followed his interests and his curiosity. He followed the energy that led him forward, and did not deny when he was called.

Jobs' story, like hundreds of people I've coached, was one of fits and starts—not a clear straightforward path. So learn to embrace that journey, the ambiguity and circuity of which are a source of excitement and fulfillment unto themselves.

Not long ago, my wife was doing a 1,000-piece jigsaw puzzle. I asked, "Sharon, how do you think you would do if I took away the box?" She looked at me quizzically, even more than usual. She responded, "Why would you do that? I need the box."

Life is like a jigsaw puzzle whose pieces have been dumped out on the dining room table but whose box with the picture of the finished puzzle on the cover is missing. So we're basically putting it together blindly, without an image to guide us toward the endpoint.

As this metaphorical puzzle encapsulates your whole existence (past, present, and future), it's larger than anything you could buy in the toy store. It's basically infinite. Each piece represents every discrete thought and action you take: every day we're brushing our teeth, we're getting up, we're working out, we're going to our job, we're making our sales calls, we're seeing family, we're reading one book or another. And we're gathering the pieces of our puzzle and we're creating that image, one by one. It happens very slowly, and if you're like most people, somewhat aimlessly.

But without the picture on the box to guide you, it would be really challenging. Frustrating even. You'd probably spin your wheels. You might try to force fit pieces or even, ultimately, give up.

So many of us move through life in this way, slowly stringing pieces together. But to what end? What does the puzzle look like as a result? We've laid out half of a purple balloon over there, the green crest of a hill over here, and who knows what this thing in the corner is shaping up to be? And after a while, even though we're making fragmentary progress, we're not doing it in the service of a fully formed vision that unites all these disparate parts into a beautiful landscape.

I'm sure you can relate. How many times have you wondered, "I did a lot this week (or month or year), but I'm not really sure what I accomplished." If your actions were not working in service of a clearly defined *what* (and the *why* and *how* to accompany it), you may feel you came up short. Of course, there is no shame in that. On the contrary, that's really how the majority—including successful people—live their lives. But it's something that should be remedied. "Should," in this case, applies to the correctness or appropriateness that this kind of change might mean for you—not the kind of "should" that means external pressure, or because a life coach wrote about it in his book. When someone is motivated to change, his or her "should" must be personally defined.

It makes perfect sense to work on the puzzle with the box art next to us, *even if we know that picture is never going to be perfectly clear,* nor is it going to remain static over time. The real jigsaw puzzle of life is not one lovely finished picture. There is no single image we are shooting for. Each of our lives/puzzles is a mosaic of individual consequential goals we have set for ourselves.

We work little by little, piece by piece, setting goals as we go; the overall image changes as we change, as our goals change, and as we deal with life on life's terms. I do not believe we begin and end with the same vision in mind. Therein lies the exciting part of being alive: it's a messy process that is rarely simple or straightforward. But it is a creative one! Our task is to make the images as clear as they possibly can be, so we can meet each new day with as much intentionality in our actions and conviction in our decisions as possible. Your jigsaw puzzle will represent the aggregate of all your goals, relationships, dreams, challenges, victories, and decisions. But you won't look back at age 75 and say, "I finished the picture I saw on the box." Instead, you will be amazed at the vast multitude of images you made, following your energy and your courage—and tapping into the power of visualization.

WE'RE ALL IN THE MOOD FOR A MELODY: FINDING YOUR PIANO MAN

You may know exactly what you were put on this earth to do. Or you may have a more nebulous idea. For me, it began with two letters penciled onto a notepad: HR.

In time, the vague idea about "human resources" would germinate into the more concrete pursuit of coaching. It took a while. But eventually, I found my Piano Man.

"What is a Piano Man?" you're probably wondering. Well, when I first arrived at business school, I was in an incredibly receptive state. I let the aperture in my mind open wide so I could take in everything, meet people, challenge long-held assumptions and embrace new ones, and see things in different ways.

I was sitting at my desk one night in the middle of orientation. I had the TV on for background noise while I dug into the reading to prepare for the next day.

Suddenly, a massive chorus of singing voices caught my ear. It was just a commercial, but it commanded all my attention. Billy Joel was touring, and they were advertising the next show with footage from a previous concert at Madison Square Garden or, as a New Yorker, what I projected to be taking place in that famous arena.

The song they used was "Piano Man," which was his first big hit, the breakthrough single that paved the way for a legendary career. It's been a mainstay on the radio since its 1973 debut—if you flipped through the radio right now, I wouldn't be surprised if you came across a station playing it. Perhaps its famous chorus is playing in your head as you read this.

At that moment in my apartment, an entire audience of nearly 20,000 people in the commercial were all joyously singing along while he played his passionate best. I had three thoughts in quick succession: first, it would be fun to go to that concert. If someone were a die-hard Billy Joel fan, being there and communing over the music with so many other fans would be something like a religious experience.

Second, what if Billy Joel had done something else with his life?

What if he'd never made a serious effort at becoming a professional musician? "Piano Man" actually came on the heels of his first record, a technical and commercial failure. What if he had thrown in the towel after that setback?

Billy Joel had enjoyed a pretty good run as an amateur boxer on the Golden Gloves circuit; what if he'd decided to go pro in that arena instead? He has said he was a good student. What if he'd played it safe and gone to college, instead of going for a record deal?

He was working in piano bars helping support his mom (a single parent), having done so since he was in high school, an undertaking that was (I imagine) as tough as it was admirable. Deciding to pursue music professionally is a daunting choice; being able to support yourself is a long shot. Becoming a star? Almost as improbable as winning the lottery.

That commercial only lasted half a minute, but it sparked an hours-long period of rumination. At one point, Billy had seen the fork in the road, and chose a path. He knew what he wanted.

The third thought I had was where I asked myself, what was *my* Piano Man? This was the one that stopped me in my tracks. A big question that was suddenly hanging over my head, and would for weeks—months and years—thereafter.

I wanted an accomplishment like that of my own. I wanted to make a huge contribution based on my abilities, my strengths, my hard work, and my willingness to seize the right opportunities. I knew I wanted to make an impact. I also knew I didn't want to swim upstream. That's tiring. Swimming against the current drains valuable energy and makes each stroke a challenge.

The catalyst for these thoughts could have been anything. The important thing was that I was listening to someone's personal masterpiece. Something *only he* could have contributed to the world.

The next day, still contemplating this notion that everyone has a "Piano Man" inside, yearning to see the daylight, I sprinted to my classroom and immediately found Greg, who eventually became my closest friend in the MBA program.

I blurted, "Greg, what's your Piano Man?"

"What the hell are you talking about?" he said. I explained to him what I'd experienced the night before, and then watched as the realization dawned in his eyes. He didn't know what his Piano Man was at that point any more than I knew mine. But we both knew we had to find one, and find our way to develop it. A treasure hunt, of sorts.

HOW TO WRITE YOUR LIFE'S GREATEST HIT

By this point in your Piano Man process, the picture formed by the infinite jigsaw puzzle is starting to emerge. It's still mostly just a pile of cardboard pieces on the dining room table of your life, but we're linking individual pieces and joining clusters of pieces with other clusters. We're ready to put forth some hypotheses about what your Piano Man, your extraordinary contribution to the world, might be. It bears repeating that although we often talk about job and career in the context of personal change, your Piano Man may have nothing to do with what you "do for a living." And it may be more than one thing. This makes sense, as people are a complex constellation of desires, interests, and goals. More often, by the time we have finalized your unique Game Plan, there are three or four interrelated or integrated goals. Let's consider the theme of the Piano Man, in terms of why, what, and how.

I'll use myself as the example again. Years ago, when I was working with a coach to figure out the next phase of my life journey, he and I, after conducting the Sources/Drains exercise, came to the conclusion that being the chief human resources officer of a Fortune

WHAT is it that you might like to do?
Your Hypotheses to Test

(Based on what matters to me, my Why, I want to):

- **Hypothesis 1:** To be a CHRO of a Fortune 500 company
- **Hypothesis 2:** To work as a Human Capital Consultant at a large consultancy
- **Hypothesis 3:** To join a boutique executive coaching firm
- **Hypothesis 4:** To launch my own company and begin coaching
- **Hypothesis 5:** To join a VC or PE firm as a Human Capital operating partner/Performance coach

Figure 5.1 Hypothesis generator.

100 company would have been my ideal position. I generated five hypotheses (Figure 5.1), as part of the "what" process and through the "how," I tested them.

Though I ultimately determined that while HR didn't quite hit the mark either, I was getting closer. And even if a hypothesis doesn't hold up to scrutiny, it's still useful because the very process of investigation often helps you uncover *the essential quality* that takes you one step closer to the truth. Even if X (e.g., heading the HR department in a major company) wasn't my Piano Man, by deconstructing it, I found that it was X's essential quality, Y, that really thrilled me. It's a little like cracking a walnut—you don't want the shell, you want the savory morsel inside, which you obtain by applying a little pressure to break through that tough exterior. My own method aims to refute, refine, and confirm hypotheses. Human Resources wasn't my fit due to a number of reasons. I studied those reasons. Layered them over the content generated from my Sources/Drains exercise, and came to understand them and what they said about me, and confirmed that HR was, indeed, not the landing place for me. I walked away having learned valuable details about myself, and they pointed me forward.

And discovering your Piano Man *is* a major break-through. That's the what, as in "what do I want to do with my life to achieve self-actualization?" There is a dynamic symbiosis between the "what," the "how," and the "why." The why is the secret ingredient that goal-setting and other "find your purpose" systems lack, and the how is the means to achieve it. Let's put it this way: the what is your vision and the why is your mission.

Harmonizing the three is one of the most exciting experiences in coaching because when they meet, it's an exhilarating organic reaction: their interplay produces heat and light that fires you up and illuminates you from within. Introspection (honestly getting to know yourself) catalyzes with action (when you believe you are worth the effort and can make things happen) to empower you to meet challenges head on, and create durable long-term change.

Fortunately, you don't have to undertake this project solo, since you have the aid of a coach by your side. In Chapter 6, I'll delve more deeply into what coaching specifically entails and how it compares to other advisory roles like therapist or mentor, so you can determine the approach that works best for you.

"If you are not doing what you love, you are wasting your time."

– Billy Joel

A Seat at the Table

Andrew Lawrence was at a career crossroad. He was an authority on creating diversity in the workplace. Even more than that, he was a world-class connector who knew exactly what every business needed, especially when it came to tapping underrepresented communities for overlooked talent. Andrew thought he knew what he wanted. The challenge was finding the right company and role.

The breadth of his professional and philanthropic experiences meant he could succeed in any number of industries or companies. He also could have stayed in his current role as a senior executive at a renowned and influential organization. But that didn't provide enough excitement or juice for him. To put it simply, Andrew wanted more.

In our coaching sessions, we created a business plan for the next phase of Andrew's career. We looked at all the industries and companies where he would be welcomed, all the potential job choices in front of him and we selected none of them. Instead, Andrew started his own entity, which immediately found itself with enough demand for him to make the leap from employee to entrepreneur.

Andrew's mission was to provide opportunities for members of underrepresented groups who were highly talented but were often overlooked for key positions. At the same time, he wanted to share his wisdom about diversity and inclusion with as many prominent businesses as possible.

It was certainly a big risk for him to go off and create something from nothing, especially given the lure of continuing on as a salary + bonus employee. The work of building his own enterprise was slow and demanding but the growth was consistent. Then came the COVID-19 pandemic and the racial reckoning that followed the murder of George Floyd.

Suddenly, corporate America "discovered" the size and importance of minority markets. No one was better positioned than Andrew to help firms identify new talent and find ways to communicate with minority groups. After nearly four years of existence, Andrew's firm had begun to create a huge shift in racial awareness in the business world. A global executive search and leadership consulting firm acquired his firm, bringing Andrew in-house and giving him an even bigger platform from which to realize his vision.

Now, Andrew helps his new organization think more holistically about how they undertake their executive searches. And they bring Andrew's expertise to their client base and find candidates from groups underrepresented in the corporate world for their searches.

Andrew and I spent endless hours talking through all the pluses and minuses of making a move like this. He made a leap, and best of all, he made the leap that most reflected what he really wanted to do. As a result, he has never looked back.

6

WHAT IS COACHING, AND WHAT IS THE VALUE OF COACHING?

Socrates and Plato. FDR and Churchill. Larry Page and Sergey Brin. From Hellenic wisdom to the Allied victory in World War II to the conception of Google, some of history's greatest achievements have been the result of partnerships.

When two people unite in an unswerving commitment to a common goal, great things emerge. Their distinct roles harmonize and their unique skills complement each other to produce exciting insights and bold actions.

Many people, especially the highly ambitious and successful, feel compelled to tackle their problems alone because they don't know how or where to ask for help, or they think they don't need it. Surely the idealization of individualism and independence plays a role, too. But in a partnership, the collaborative strength of both parties adds up to a whole that is greater than the sum of their parts.

Coaching is a specialized kind of partnership, and my role as a coach is to meet you on equal terms, not as an authority figure. I serve as an advocate who empowers you to achieve your goals, whether that means fixing something that's broken or missing in your life, or allowing you to build on your current success so you can continue thriving in your next endeavor. (More and more, coaching is focusing on the latter.) True and effective coaching is not directive, it is reflective.

In this chapter, I'll talk about what coaching is and is not, and how it compares to other supportive types of relationships.

COACHING VERSUS THERAPY

The function of coaches and therapists[1] are sometimes conflated, and they do have several things in common. Both tend to involve a lot of talking face-to-face about your desires and fears, about what exhilarates you, and what holds you back. Both depend on trust between both parties. You yourself may benefit from therapy, from coaching, or from both (as I have). But you must understand each in order to figure out what suits you and your needs.

I'd argue that the main distinction between coaching and therapy is that therapy tends to be backwards-looking, while coaching looks more toward the future.

There are myriad therapeutic schools and techniques, so I don't want to generalize too much, but for the most part, therapy is predicated on analyzing the patient's past as a means of understanding their present: this may include their experiences during their formative

---

[1] In this case, I'm using "therapist" the way people usually understand it—psychologist or psychiatrist—but other types of therapists who may not be licensed psychologists exist, too, such as marriage counselors or social workers.

years of childhood and adolescence, painful events that have shaped their psyche as adults, and long-festering issues that still hold them back from achieving their fully realized self.

One reason coaches don't get into the thorny issues that psychologists and psychiatrists help people work through—childhood trauma, long-running, deep-seated conflict with parents and other authority figures, mental illness, etc.—is because we're just not trained for that. It's a different set of practices for a different set of needs. When trauma does come up in the coaching session, I usually reorient the discussion toward the present and the future, toward actions that one can take to overcome whatever fear, anxiety, or self-doubt lingers as the result of past hardships.

I also recognize there are certain things I know and certain things I don't; that my training, while extensive, does not cover all areas of human need. Nor is it designed to address all problems that may emerge during the client-coach dialogue. I do make referrals to therapists if I sense the client can benefit from it. Therapy, of course, is not in opposition to coaching, and the two practices are not an either/or proposition. Some of the best partnerships, those that yield the most benefit, happen when the client sees a therapist and also works with me.

Certainly, there is value in the retrospection of therapy, especially for people who are working through trauma. But while the past is immutable, the present is still a blank canvas, one that can be painted any way you like, and that's where coaches really shine. My clients come to me because they have certain desires about the future, irrespective of their past—they are eager "to go confidently in the direction of your dreams," as Thoreau famously put it.

The coach doesn't hold the paintbrush or choose the palette; the coach provides the easel, giving the clients the support and space they need to take the images in their mind and manifest them on canvas: these works of art that are their life's work. That vision takes shape on the canvas.

The relationship is similar to that of the personal trainer and the person getting in shape at the gym. The trainer is the expert on the *process*, and the client is the expert on what he/she wants to achieve—lose weight, get more toned, lower blood pressure, prepare for a season of tennis, etc. And how much of the weight does the trainer lift? In most cases, none. In this partnership, process (coach) meets content (client).

The magic of coaching happens because we are looking forward and not looking backward, and this allows us to achieve breakthroughs—sometimes in the first hour—that might never have come up in therapy. A trained coach can help elicit some striking self-discoveries, sometimes very quickly. On various occasions a client has told me, "I've been in therapy for 10 years and we have never even talked about these things. And after one session here, I already understand what I need to get on the right track."

What you've done or not done before today does not define you. Instead, your life is forged by the actions you take from here on out. This is the inflection point. It is a moment that signifies a change in the individual's own "right direction." At the inflection point, the very next steps a person takes will bring a noticeable change with positive energy—as if having wings for the first time. It is a dramatic, remarkable, and critical turning point. The coach stands with the client at this point, and helps him identify present challenges. As the client takes action, he sees and feels results, and realizes the power of his transition. Challenges are turned into victories, as the client grows more and more mindful with his journey. The future takes precedence over the past.

I am not setting up coaching in opposition to therapy but merely stating that while there is some overlap (and even some cross-pollination of ideas), they are distinct practices that address different needs. I am an advocate for therapy. As a coach, I see immense progress in those I partner with who also are in therapy. In particular, I'm a big believer in Viktor Frankl's *logotherapy*, which posits that the purpose of life, and the secret to well-being, is the personal pursuit for *meaning*.

Frankl was an incredible figure, a Holocaust survivor who lost his wife in the death camps; he understood the extremes of suffering the way few people do. Instead of emerging from that terrible ordeal with a nihilistic and meaningless view of the world, Frankl channeled his experiences into a school of therapy that would help others find value and fulfillment in their existential quest. The seminal (and aptly named) book he authored just after the war, *Man's Search for Meaning*,[2] defined that search as "1) creating a work or doing a deed; (2) by experiencing something or encountering someone; and (3) by the attitude we take toward unavoidable suffering." Some of Frankl's ideas I've incorporated into my own coaching practice, especially when it comes to finding your "what" and exploring the "why" that drives it. If one has a clear idea of the why, he can work through almost any how, Frankl wrote (paraphrasing Nietzsche).

Another key distinction between coaching and therapy is that therapists—psychologists or psychiatrists—are usually medical professionals and, hence, their training is fundamentally different from the training coaches undergo. Medicine is a branch of science that serves to protect the health of, and rectify problems with, the physical body and mind.

---

[2] Frankl, V.E. (1959 English edition). *Man's Search for Meaning: An Introduction to Logotherapy.* New York: Beacon Press.

Coaching is certainly concerned with mental and physical health, and the coaching conversation can be, and often is when conducted properly, therapeutic. However, the outlook is less one of applying scientific practices to ailments and disorders and more based on empowering individuals to affect changes or maintain what is working for them through a process of self-discovery that affirms their own willpower and agency. Doctors can heal you, but coaches enable you to heal or improve yourself. I use the term "heal" loosely in the context of coaching because it's not just a matter of correcting a deficiency; in fact, most of my clients seek my partnership not because they're dealing with a crisis but because they're doing well, yet still desire support to help them advance to the next level of personal, professional, or emotional development.

DIRECTIVE VERSUS REFLECTIVE

Coaches should also not be confused with "consultants," in all their various iterations. Consultants hired to evaluate and improve some aspect of your personal or professional life take a *directive* approach: they'll analyze the situation, diagnose a problem, and prescribe remedies. This protocol is similar to that of a physician, and for matters of physiological health, a directive approach (telling you what to do and how to do it) is probably the right method. If you go to a doctor with a sprained ankle, she is going to tell you to ice, rest, wrap, and elevate. Or if you have a heart condition, your cardiologist will recommend you quit smoking, lose weight, and exercise. It's very matter of fact. And in many instances, the prescription is not followed. The directive approach has its place. But it lacks in triggering motivation from within.

In contrast, coaches (and therapists, too) utilize a more *reflective* strategy, wherein we don't tell clients what to do or think, but provide a framework that allows them to make discoveries themselves; we equip them with cognitive and emotional tools they can use to act on those discoveries. Our role is to hold a mirror up to the client's life, enabling a dynamic process of introspection that inspires the client to take action on their terms and by their own initiative. There is no singular prescription or remedy, and the client is active in pursuing the change he or she wants. There is no waiting around for the ankle to mend.

The International Coach Federation[3] provides a widely accepted definition of coaching that neatly articulates this concept: "partnering with clients in a

---

[3] ICF is one of a handful of governing bodies in the coaching world. They work to uphold coaching standards, provide training and certification, with a code of ethics and conduct review. I'm not endorsing it here, but I do think their definition is apt.

thought-provoking and creative process that inspires them to maximize their personal and professional potential." We don't judge, diagnose, or order around. On the GPS highway, we're the guardrails that keep you safely on the road, moving toward your destination, rather than the traffic cop issuing commands and doling out tickets. And coaches will not tell you what to pursue. That is driven by you.

Why is a reflective tack preferable to a directive one? Well, a breakthrough has more consequence if it emerges from your own mental and emotional labor—the output of soul-searching, self-reflection, and planning. Furthermore, coaches, while astute, are not some bastion of inner esoteric knowledge that we reveal only when our clients have solved three riddles, jumped through an arbitrary number of hoops, answered X number of questions—or anything like that. We're not gurus waiting to give the secrets of life to the curious disciple who climbs up to our temple on the mountaintop.

A good coach can certainly offer a wealth of knowledge and expertise, but that doesn't mean he necessarily *knows* what is right for the client in a given moment. The coach is not the guru; she's more akin to the Sherpa who partners with you and guides you to the summit. (You have determined where you want to go. What would be meaningful to you. The Sherpa increases the chances of making it so.) Then, in your own moment of great surprise, you often find there is no bearded, enlightened temple master who can give you all the answers. The answers, you discover along with your partner-coach, were within you all along.

In other words, you identify what mountain you want to climb, and you go on that journey with the coach as you undertake the trip to the top. It's a partnership, yes, but you still do all the work. The coach is holding the mirror, and proverbially improving your reflection.

This dynamic is one of the great aspects of coaching. There is an equal balance of power in the partnership so the client feels secure as he works his way forward. Coaching empowers the client to locate his own truths from within and helps nurture client confidence.

Therapy, in fact, is similar in that therapists generally don't tell patients what to do or how to live. They don't "give advice," but they do guide the dialogue in a way that reveals insights about one's self and the world, clarifying the patient's understanding of his circumstances and thus enabling better decision-making amidst the manifold choices and paths of action available.

COACHING IS FOR WINNERS

I don't know if I'd say this is "the golden age of coaching," but the industry has undergone a kind of a renaissance in recent years, as more and more people (and companies) are discovering the life-changing benefits of partnering with a coach, and as the reputation of coaching itself is evolving. In the United States alone, $1 billion is spent annually on coaching (up from $700 million in 2011), with an estimated 53,300 coaches operating worldwide (with two-thirds of them in the United States)—an increase of almost 6,000 over the last decade.[4]

For a long time, coaching, especially in the corporate world, was seen as a corrective measure, maybe even a last resort, for troubled employees. In the worst case, coaches were brought on mostly to help the firm protect itself from liability as it made preparations to terminate an irredeemable employee.

This was a bleak state of affairs that reduced the whole coaching experience to an HR charade, and reflected none of the synergy between coach and client/partner (or between coach, client/partner, and organization). It's fortunate for all parties that the model has reformed, and that many more people now appreciate the power of coaching for both the individual and the organization.

Coaching has gone from a stigma—a scarlet letter C—to a badge of honor. Today, instead of being used

---

[4] LaRosa, J. (2018). U.S. personal coaching industry tops $1 billion, and growing, MarketResearch.com (12 February). https://blog.marketresearch.com/us-personal-coaching-industry-tops-1-billion-and-growing.

as a stopgap for underperforming employees, coaching is typically employed by organizations to turbocharge high achievers or to develop high-potential talent that will benefit the company for years to come. Your top performers generate the greatest value, and so pairing them with a coach is, correctly, regarded as an investment in the company's future rather than a last-ditch attempt to save a problematic employee.

Indeed, most of my clients are stellar performers who want and need a boost to push them to an even higher level—both in and out of the office. That's where I step in to be a thought partner to help get things done. I am a mentor, a solicitor, a consultant, a sort of director, and an advisor. The coach can ultimately be whatever you need and want him or her to be.

Look around, and you'll see that the most extraordinary people have a coach on the sidelines, quietly supporting their stardom. Pro athletes, naturally, have a coach. Warren Buffett had a coach—Columbia Business School professor and legendary finance author Benjamin Graham.

Even the leaders at Google and hundreds of other luminaries in Silicon Valley have been coached—many by Bill Campbell, who was a legendary figure.

A former Major League Baseball All-Star player turned entrepreneur, and one of my clients, once told me, "Coaches have always been able to bring out the best in me, and have helped me bring my game to the highest levels. I don't understand why more business executives don't have coaches."

THE PROCESS

We've been talking about the theoretical underpinnings of coaching, but let's get into the nuts and bolts. You are the expert of your own life, and I, the coach, am the trained expert on the research-based processes that will, as we work in collaboration, improve your life.

At the outset of the partnership, the client and I identify what we want to accomplish during our time together and, specifically, what will make it valuable for them. We strive to meet every other week, though this is not rigid and depends on the circumstances. In the first month, which is heavy on information gathering, we may do three or four sessions, which serve as a kind of diagnostic phase. After we establish our foundation there is the co-creation of the Game Plan System, and then we execute the GPS.

It's a nonstop partnership, meaning that I'm always available for my clients. Why? Because the fascinating chemistry of coaching doesn't just happen in session. Our fortnightly meetings percolate into between sessions, so you may be walking down the street and have a sudden epiphany or burning question that you *need* to speak to me about. I don't want it to wait until the next coaching session. These moments are crucial and should be cultivated when they arise; breakthroughs are powerful but can be ephemeral or delicate, hence the value of the always-on approach.

I don't begin a relationship with the expectation that it will last indefinitely, and I'm happy to reach an endpoint where clients say, "Matt, thank you. I've accomplished what I set out to accomplish with your help!" Or, "I've made the changes I sought when I first came to you, and I believe I'm ready to conclude." After all, the nature of the GPS is not circular, but linear: from Point A to Point B.

I have found that the complexion of the relationship changes naturally. It may have commenced at the start of a new job, so onboarding was the focus, but then it transitioned to something else. Flexibility is a strength of the process, and this reminds us of the fact that coaching is something somebody could benefit from all the time, even as their situation evolves. I have been working with my own coach for 10 years.

DOWNSIDES AND RISKS

The explosion of coaching's popularity in recent years has produced a proliferation of coaches of various stripes and levels of proficiency. For now, coaching is largely unregulated, such that anyone can call himself a coach, kind of like anyone can call himself a "financial advisor," even though only Certified Financial Planners and those with similar certifications have passed the rigorous training and exam regimen for earning that distinction.

Fortunately, organizations such as the ICF and prestigious coaching programs at Columbia, Georgetown, and Berkeley help reinforce the professionalization of the industry, which continues to develop. Codes of conduct and standardization of best practices benefit both coaches and clients alike, assuring that good coaches are partnered with clients in need while discouraging untrained persons from misrepresenting themselves as qualified coaches.

Therefore, make sure your coach has actually been trained as a coach. I feel training is essential not only for quality, but also for client peace of mind. Above all, training gives you a professional backbone for having the ability to really listen on multiple levels; it teaches you how to ask the really important questions, and how to do the right kind of framing. Certification also entails a level of accountability—not just an individual operating on his or her own "good ideas." Moreover, there is the actual respect for the importance of the craft of coaching. Perhaps someone might be a decent coach without formal training, but the fact that she commits so much time, energy, and money to the training process shows how serious it is to her. The client brings serious and sensitive life issues in good confidence, and that's not something to be taken casually. When building a house, you want a licensed construction company.

Although untrained individuals may be acting in good faith, they're not actually coaches (even if they call themselves that)—they tend to be more advisors or consultants. The problem with leaning too heavily on consultants is that the power dynamic is tilted and the explicit goal in coaching of *empowering the client* toward his or her own self-actualization is missing, so that the client becomes dependent on the consultant to "solve the client's problems." A good coach never wants her client to lose one's self-sufficiency and agency.

Finally, a good coach strategically directs the conversation but he does not dominate it—he keeps the focus on the client. Generally, a coach should not talk about himself. An exception would be if the client specifically *asks* the coach to do so; for instance, if the coach has direct experience with a problem the client is working on. As the saying goes, a gentleman is someone who knows how to play the bagpipes, but doesn't.

In keeping with the extended metaphor of the road trip and the GPS, in coaching, unlike therapy or consultancy, the client is the driver. The coach is the passenger. By way of reflection and a series of conversations, the client determines the desired destination that is then programmed into the GPS.

It's the client who remains behind the wheel, shifting gears, moving forward. The rearview mirror doesn't warrant more than a passing glance. A coach may ask: "What worked well in a particular instance, and how can you can apply to the current situation?" Analyzing the past is the job of therapists—and there can be great value in that. But as a coach, I am pointing you toward the future—the endless, open highway of your life, which can be so exhilarating to drive on when you know where you're going and have someone next to you to ensure you get there. Imagine driving that car, taking in the spectacular scenery and details of all you see. You have an ultimate destination, and you are fully engaged in the feel of the ride. Equipped with your map and your copilot, you know you'll arrive on time—and in style. You aren't thinking about the past, nor are you anxious about the future. Knowing where you're going, you can appreciate every mile of the drive. This is how our future-oriented focus helps us be more conscious in the present. Nothing can distract you from this moment.

But before any long road journey commences, before you even turn the ignition, you have to know your starting point. In Chapter 7, we'll look at the process of assessing your current state in life, which you must do before developing and executing a plan to tackle the future.

Can Introverts and Extroverts Get Along at Work?

Anyone who's ever been involved in a corporate acquisition knows that the hardest problem isn't negotiating the deal. It's integrating team members from two often radically different cultures, melding their characters and abilities into a new entity that creates success far beyond what either of the prior companies could have done on their own.

Everyone involved in acquisitions also knows that the potential for things going south very quickly, for mergers and acquisitions to fail, for disappointment, and, ultimately, lawsuits and catastrophe, is high.

This was the problem facing Arjan Batra, the CEO of a leading software firm. I ran into Arjan at our 20-year business school reunion. He said, "Matt, we just acquired a company—different culture, different location. We're having some integration issues and we want to have an off-site.

"I want you to come to Nashville, where we're flying everybody in from the two different teams. There'll be about 25 from our team and 20 from theirs. I need you to straighten this out."

So down to Nashville I went. You don't have to acquire another company to have issues arise when people who communicate differently and see the world differently are asked to work together. Arjan's firm provides software to the financial services industry. The last thing they could afford was any disruption to the development, installation, or updating of their products and services as they assimilated the newly acquired company. So that was the problem I faced.

At the off-site, I began by administering personality assessments to trigger self-awareness in each of the attendees and help them better understand each other. I had administered this tool ahead of time and then shared the results with the group. I explained that the assessment identifies different personality types, and I did some exercises with individuals in front of the whole group that accentuated the unique qualities of those types.

Let's say Jane is extroverted and Pete is more of an introvert. I gave Jane and Pete a business scenario and let them talk through, in front of the entire team, how they saw the problem and how they would solve it. To say the least, Jane and Pete had radically different approaches to the same problem!

Each explained their own natural responses. Their team members had a lot of aha moments. They were saying things like, "Okay, that's why I tend to do that!" or "That's why John down the hall does what he does," or "So that's why Amy tends to use analogies and metaphors!"

The result for the team was a much better understanding of themselves as individuals, and a much deeper understanding of their teammates. It brought people together, and the two groups closer. Lots of smiling and lots of laughing came along with these realizations, a sharp change from the tension that had pervaded the group prior to the exercise.

Ever since, the company's members consistently reference their personality profiles—they actually appear on the signature lines of their emails. So it might say, Jerry Larson, ENFP, or Cathy Jones, INTJ.

By having fun with differences between team members, and coming to understand, rather than being put off by them, the group came together and became truly one organization.

7

WHERE
ARE YOU NOW?

Imagine you're waiting in the exam room of your doctor's office. The room is silent but for the crinkle of exam table paper beneath you and the hum of the fluorescent lights above. You hope the doc arrives soon—you've been experiencing some mysterious physical pains and you're looking to get some answers.

Finally, after a long wait, in walks the doctor. But before you can even explain your symptoms, he gives you the once-over and announces, "Looks like lupus." He tosses a prescription paper at you and tells you to call him in a week.

"Sorry, Doctor," you say, "shouldn't you run some tests? I didn't even explain my symptoms!" But by then, he's already out the door.

This would be a weird way to assess someone's health condition (bordering on malpractice!). The first step to proper treatment is always a well-reasoned diagnosis. Coaching is no different. In coaching, as in medicine, there can be no prognosis without a diagnosis, and there can be no diagnosis without a careful evaluation of the patient's current state. This means that I listen carefully to my clients.

This diagnostic process is the first phase of coaching, and, as mentioned in Chapter 6, provides the foundation for the entire engagement. Patiently, I gather thorough information about where the client stands now in various aspects of his life, and what he hopes to achieve. This is how we devise the Game Plan System, which is the second phase. The third phase is executing the plan, which I'll discuss later.

Unfortunately, many coaches rush this all-important first diagnostic step, but investing this time at the beginning makes for a better coaching experience over the long term. Putting in the hard work at the start will pay dividends for the months and years to come. We look to go slow in order to go fast. Doing right from the very beginning ensures we are prepared for the opportunities that lie ahead.

After conducting thousands of preliminary discussions, I've fine-tuned the process to systematically and consistently produce the needed information that forms the solid foundation for the coaching partnership while remaining flexible enough to account for the unique circumstances, life experience, and desires of each client.

THE ART OF LISTENING

It all starts with a few simple yet powerful questions. This is the starting point of a long and fruitful dialogue that extends over the course of the engagement as we develop and carry out your Game Plan. This constitutes the "informal information gathering" part of the diagnosis, which is, depending on the unique needs and desires of the client, sometimes supplemented by

nal information gathering" in the form of behav- assessments.

There are a series of initial questions I ask each client to start the information information gathering process. *To prepare for the first meeting, I have new clients answer the following questions before we meet for the first session.* About your life and career:

> What are you most proud of?
>
> What has been your biggest disappointment?
>
> What is the complement or acknowledgment you hear most often about yourself?
>
> What words describe you at your best?
>
> What words describe you when you are at less than your best?
>
> What activities have meaning for you?
>
> Imagine you can have one wish fulfilled. What one thing would you change?

About coaching you:

> What will make this coaching relationship rewarding for you?
>
> What approaches encourage or motivate you?
>
> What approaches discourage or de-motivate you?
>
> How will you know you are receiving value from this coaching relationship?
>
> What else would you like me to know about you?

During the preliminary conversation, the client and I discuss the answers to try to get at the heart of what makes her tick, what she values deeply, and what she seeks to get out of life and work.

While it is indeed a *dialogue,* the client does most of the talking. I listen and ask follow-up questions, as needed. Deep listening, and really hearing, is something of a lost art in our society; it's striking how many accomplished individuals have never really had the opportunity to sit down and talk freely about their desires, dreams, wishes, regrets, and achievements. Deep listening is what certified life coaches are trained to practice. It's powerful because it gives the client a chance to expound on topics they may never have talked about, to a nonjudgmental listener who will synthesize what they're saying into a life-changing Game Plan System.

I don't ask an endless barrage of questions. Simpler is better. Sometimes certain questions hit the mark so well that they generate enough momentum to carry the conversation to the end. In these sessions, I just let the client speak while I take notes, allowing the life-changing magic of introspection to do its work in opening up new perspectives and new ranges of action.

The coach's job is not only listening to the client's words but also deconstructing the *subtext* that underlies what is said—to get past the surface of spoken language to penetrate that deeper, more meaningful layer, where the real truth emerges.

You don't have to be a coach to recognize that when people speak, there are multiple levels of meaning that coexist. Often, what they say and what they truly feel or believe are often in conflict, in a way even the speaker may not recognize. One powerful tool that coaches often use is the rephrasing of a client's statement. This allows the individual to hear his own thoughts, which can clarify patterns and unlock a new sense of understanding. It's like seeing the same object photographed from a different angle. The words themselves provide clues or signposts that direct us to the answer, but they're not necessarily the answer itself. As a coach, you have to dig a little bit to clarify what they're getting at.

For example, I was recently talking with a client about her plans to run a marathon, which is an important goal for her. As we probed her motivations for undertaking the grueling task of training and preparing for this 26.2-mile run, our guided conversation helped her discover that it wasn't just about the marathon, per se. Sure, running is an activity she enjoys, but what drives her is the desire to accomplish a feat of great physical and mental strenuousness—and those feelings are connected with her personal development. Her family is also involved, so that too factors into the appeal—it is a challenge she can undertake with the people closest to her. In addition, there was an emotional connection to the city to which she was returning to run the marathon, after several years of being away.

Invariably, life presents us with other plans. Friction points emerge. In this case, COVID-19 forced the cancellation of the marathon in October 2020. Was all that preparation a waste of time? Of course not.

Though she was initially dejected, we revisited the reasons for her wanting to participate in the marathon and we discussed what she could do to reproduce that same feeling of satisfaction and accomplishment. Since we had already talked extensively about her reasons for signing up for the event and what it meant personally (the why), we had a strong foundation to work with to find a suitable "replacement."

Ultimately, she came to see that it wasn't about the marathon at all. The real benefit came from a broader, deeper understanding of her own psychology and values. That insight has implications for long beyond the moment when she crosses the finish line.

A coach's ability to diagnose where a client stands by exploring the subtext is similar to how doctors are able to deduce that symptoms in one part of the body are indicative of a problem in another. For instance, in baseball, pitchers who deal with shoulder pain often modify their throwing motion, dropping their shoulder below the parallel plane, which may temporarily alleviate the strain on the shoulder. But it now exerts extra pressure on the elbow. They complain to the team orthopedist that their elbow is hurting, but in fact the origin of the problem is with the shoulder.

The root of the problem sometimes lies even deeper. Someone may be unhappy in his job, only to find that the dissatisfaction is an expression of unmet needs at home. If he had expected his work to distract him or fill in a certain gap, and it's not—we need to understand what that need for distraction, or the gap, represents. Problems like this surface during the preliminary coach-client conversation, and the resolve is worked on over the next few weeks/months and/or years, together.

Another example: clients sometimes say things like, "I need a coach because I'd really like to double my income next year." I acknowledge that's important to you but I don't merely take it at face value; together, we work to discover what's driving that goal. And as you might expect, financial goals are rarely just "about the money," or income for income's sake. There's usually a more pressing interest beneath that, whereby the money is a means to an unrelated end, or a stand-in for some other lack in their life.

In one such conversation, I asked the client what they thought was the value of doubling her and her husband's income. "I want to buy a vacation home," she said.

"And what is important to you about buying a vacation home?" I continued.

"So that my husband and I can spend more time together, away from work and the stress of daily life."

"Okay, tell me more about the stress you feel." Then, I might ask, "Where might the vacation home be? What are some of the activities you would like to do there? What does the idea of a vacation home mean to you? What do you need a vacation *from*? How might you incorporate more 'vacation' activities into your current life, and feel relief and freedom?" And so on. Looking into the elements of her answers, we would understand how she came to the conclusion of needing a larger salary to finally be happy. Or, that a vacation home represented her happiness.

And it continues in this fashion. Just a few well-timed follow-up questions have already taken us from "I want to make more money" to more fundamental, even profound issues of love, family, meaning, and autonomy (in this case, autonomy over one's own time). So in this way the diagnostic process allows you to explore your own motives and wishes in ways that later lead to important, exhilarating discoveries about the what, why, and how that have eluded you.

But don't think that coaches just sit in the chair and ask smart questions. Coaches listen carefully and nonjudgmentally, but not uncritically—our role is to process what you're saying, and, together, find the signal among the noise. As I have said, what people think (or say) they want is not actually what they want. When I, as a coach, point this out, it can lead to a lot of epiphanies, sometimes life-altering ones.

You may have noticed that I didn't ask my client, "Why do you want to buy a vacation home?" Questions that start with "why" are generally omitted. So, for example, if you said, "I feel like I'm spinning my wheels at work," I wouldn't respond with, "Why do you feel that way?" I might say, "Let's look at one of your days and go through it." Getting specific is important. When we shine a light, it is often revelatory to ask, "In what way does that feeling present itself when you're going about each day?" or "How does that affect your daily life?" Starting the question with the word "why" is limiting in scope and can put somebody on the defensive. By phrasing it differently, the client is invited to answer from a different perspective, without putting the reason ("why") front and center.

One of the most powerful questions I ask is, "What are you most proud of?" Many people have never considered this head-on. And the answers are illuminating, especially because we often find that our greatest source of pride, our strongest sense of self-satisfaction, appears in areas of life outside of work, or in other realms where we spend most of our time. It also gets at one's values—what they hold most dear. These values tend to be a stable, unifying force in one's life over the long term, so we can look to tap into them now, and in the future. How can we replicate that profound feeling of gratification in the future? Remember: coaching is about today, going forward.

The question about pride is emblematic of the interview strategy as a whole; the conversation is conducted through a positive lens that emphasizes strengths and achievements (what has worked for them) without concerning ourselves about weaknesses and failures (what hasn't worked). We're not fixing a problem that emerged from some past oversight or failure; we're concentrating the totality of their abilities on an actionable plan that connects to the true self. This realizes a certain vision of the future they haven't been able to put into practice on their own.

For example, one of the assessments I give is the "Values in Action Survey of Character Strengths," developed by Dr. Martin Seligman, one of the founders of the Positive Psychology movement. This assessment, as the name implies, gauges your strengths. We keep it really positive and it resonates quite strongly.

Positivity is the guiding principle not simply because it "feels good" to avoid negative feedback or because we're trying to sweep shortcomings under the rug, but because there is evidence that negative feedback can be counterproductive.

Psychologists have long recognized that negative emotions have a stronger effect on us than positive ones, so a dose of favorable feedback does not negate an equal measure of criticism. In fact, negative feedback, even if it's done in good faith, is often perceived by the recipient as an attack, which triggers the fight-or-flight response in the autonomic nervous system. As Richard Boyatzis explains, "Arousal of strong negative emotions. . .inhibits access to existing neural circuits and invokes cognitive, emotional, and perceptual impairment."[1] In other words, people don't learn from criticism—instead, they react defensively, shutting down and tuning out.

One might counter that while feedback couched in harsh words is detrimental, constructive criticism is still effective. However, the very notion of constructive feedback is dubious. In the *Harvard Business Review,* Marcus Buckingham and Ashley Goodall write, "Telling people what we think of their performance doesn't help them thrive and excel, and telling people how we think they should improve actually *hinders* learning." One

[1] Boyatzis, R. (2011). Neuroscience and leadership: the promise of insights. *Ivey Business Journal* (January/February). https://iveybusinessjournal.com/publication/neuroscience-and-leadership-the-promise-of-insights/.

problem is that, "humans are unreliable raters of other humans." For abstract, highly subjective areas of activity (of the type performed by top-level corporate executives or members of the professional class), the capacity for anyone objectively assessing another's conduct in an unbiased and productive fashion is more limited than we would like to admit.[2] Feedback is, the authors argue, ineffectual at best and harmful at worst—and why a coaching methodology that gets at one's "highlight reel" and rooted in Positive Psychology rather than finding flaws and describing deficits is preferable.

This is important to understand, as the high-powered executive sitting across from you in the boardroom may not be as self-assured as he or she projects outwardly. I've worked with many top performers who each day wrestle with "impostor syndrome," the psychological condition in which you feel, despite all evidence to the contrary, that your success has been undeserved, accidental, or owed to sheer dumb luck, and that at any minute you'll be unmasked as a "phony."

This is an irrational fear that is precipitated by the high-pressure environment in which highly successful people operate, especially as they climb the ladder

---

[2] Buckingham, M. and Goodall, A. (2019). The feedback fallacy. *Harvard Business Review* (March-April). https://hbr.org/2019/03/the-feedback-fallacy.

toward the top and are shouldered with an increasing number of responsibilities and tasks beyond their usual area of focus. They can start to feel like their handle on things is slipping, and they're only feigning they are in control while inwardly wondering if they can manage the next set of challenges.

If there is a silver lining to impostor syndrome, it is that, ironically, it tends to manifest in people who are actually very good at what they do. Their lack of confidence is the product of a certain perfectionism, a ceaseless drive to excel at whatever task they're given. As a coach, this drive gives us something to work with, so that instead of ruminating on why those "impostor" feelings exist, we shift the conversation to what we can do about it. How can we utilize that drive and convert the self-doubting energy behind the impostor feeling into a newfound confidence?

GETTING INPUT FROM OTHERS: THE 360-DEGREE VIEW

In some instances, for certain clients, especially corporate executives who are managing a team of people, we supplement the information gathering process by bringing other stakeholders into the fold, including colleagues, bosses, direct reports, and others—people who know the client well and can offer additional perspectives to complement the client's own self-insight.

A lot of coaches use web-based tools or just email a diagnostic questionnaire for this part of the process, but I prefer a face-to-face interview or at least a phone call or video conference, which are more dynamic and personal than an emailed list of questions.

I interview each stakeholder for half an hour, asking a preselected series of questions that focus on themes the client/partner wants to explore: improving communication, evaluating the effectiveness of a certain management style, etc.

While it may seem odd to approach your associates (or your own boss) and ask them to be interviewed by your coach, these stakeholders recognize that such a request is made in a spirit of continuous improvement and development, and they're almost always eager to help.

The 360 has benefits that go beyond the coaching process and can actually improve an executive's engagement with the people he works with: it can be a great way to establish new relationships, strengthen the connective tissue in existing ones, or mend fences, as needed. It also has great practical utility for execs who are moving into a new role or new department where they haven't gotten a chance to really know the people they'll be working with.

Without a doubt, there is a right way and a wrong way to undertake the 360. One top-level manager hired me because she had undergone a disastrous 360 with her previous employer. Instead of providing revelatory insights, it made the subject of the inquiry defensive and did not produce the positive change that was sought.

The positive schema of my strength-based approach avoids such outcomes. I don't query your colleagues and supervisors about any flaws or faults you may have; I give them the chance to talk about your assets and attributes. For example, "When is she at her best?" "What does she do well that you would like her to continue doing?" This positive framing yields better results for all parties.

Following is an actual interview guide we used for the managing partner (CEO) of my largest client. I don't always use all of these questions, but this guide will give you a clear sense of what the 360-degree process is meant to elicit.

Interview Guide for Paul Martland

- What is Paul really good at doing? What are his greatest strengths?
- Tell me about a specific time when Paul was at his best. (Project, meeting, deal, etc.) Ask for another example, if time.

- What do you want Paul to do even more of? What else?
- What are the specific functions that Paul focuses on? What else could he be doing?
- What could Paul do to continue growing the firm? How else could Paul benefit the firm?
- What is the single best thing that can come out of the coaching partnership with Paul?
- What advice do you have for Paul?
- What else would you like to share? What haven't I asked?
- To provide the most benefit in the coaching partnership for Paul, what advice do you have for Matt in working with him?

THE NEXT STEPS

Few people are used to speaking about themselves so authentically and candidly. Just being heard and listened to is energizing, liberating, and refreshing. It's a chance to dig deep within yourself and answer some of the substantial existential questions that perhaps you've been pondering for years, in quiet solitude—or maybe you've never been asked them at all, and engaging with these questions for the first time is revelatory.

And, sure, it can be uncomfortable. Even though everything is conducted through a positive lens, the process can still involve confronting difficult emotional themes such as unfulfilled desire, regret, fear, self-doubt, feelings of being misplaced or out of joint, or wrestling with that malaise of "quiet desperation" discussed earlier.

It is deeply enriching and energizing to unburden yourself of these thoughts with someone who will not only listen nonjudgmentally, but also help you process them into a life-changing plan for action.

Following the information gathering, the notes from the 360 interviews, behavioral assessments, and one-on-one discussions are synthesized with the client into a document that serves as the jumping off point for the coaching engagement. It's not a verbose academic report; it's a clear summary of the themes we've identified thus far. After the client has a chance to digest it, we sit down together and go through it.

At this point, it's less about "what" we find and more about the "so what?" What are the implications? Data in and of itself is not useful unless it provides a path. The reports aren't meant to be shelved 10 minutes after we go over them. It's an actionable, living document that identifies where you are and where you want to go, and offers hints on how to get there.

You may have seen similar self-diagnostic tools, such as "The Wheel of Life." Since life isn't as smooth as a wheel, the idea of putting together a puzzle makes more sense to me. The Purpose Puzzle, depicted in Figure 7.1, is a key part of the current state assessment process as it provides a snapshot of where the client is at across multiple dimensions, and where they'd like to be (the desired future state).

My approach is a little different. In this Purpose Puzzle, you numerically evaluate 9 pieces (as it is actually a puzzle): the core elements of your personal, family, social, professional, and intellectual life, along with spiritual needs and physical health. Then you compare the present state to a potential or desired state. What does "Today" look like and what might you want "Tomorrow" to look like?

Taking inventory helps you assess what is important to you, and what changes need to occur to get where

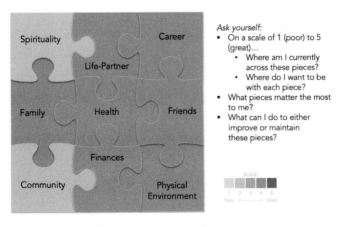

Figure 7.1   The Purpose Puzzle.

you want to be. The exercise also clarifies those areas that *are* working for you, and the things that are important and a source of joy, which you'd like to maintain. For each client who comes to me in search of a transition is one who is just looking for guidance on how to thrive in a current role. Coaching isn't always a gut renovation of the whole house. Sometimes it's just a kitchen remodel. Or maybe all your life needs is a fresh coat of paint—an understanding of what's driving you and how you might be seeing things in the day-to-day (in fact, rarely will a client need change that is a complete 180).

You already know my own story. I had done well in the corporate world, and by the time I reached an executive position at MTV Networks, I was enjoying a lifestyle that on paper seemed pretty cool: title, financial security, fun workplace, cool parties, tickets to the VMAs, all of these things. But even as I kept hitting goals, the work was missing the deeper significance I was craving. I felt like every step I took was one step I wasn't taking somewhere else, somewhere I needed to be—but where? And what did that look like? I didn't know how to articulate it. That's when I started working with my coach.

The point, of course, is not that one path is better than another, but that everyone must find his or her own. So my story is different than my clients' stories, which is different than yours, which is different than everyone else's, and that's the beautiful truth behind all of this. Answering the simple question "where are you now?" is the starting point of one's own path.

We are different and have different stories. And mentors, advisors, friends, and family members often provide advice based on what *they* would do. Coaches leave themselves out. Instead they focus on the client. Their agenda. What really matters to them. How they see the world. Not how I see the world or what I would do or what has heart for me.

Until now, you may have struggled with feeling you are on a path that doesn't really feel like your own. It may make sense on paper, or seem like the kind of life you *should* follow, but you're still dreaming about the possibility of something else, something different. If only. . . if only what? Those three words pack tremendous power. If only what? Well, what's stopping you?

In the next chapter, I'll lift the veil from the "shoulds" (what we *should* do). The shoulds tend to dominate our life for so long that we lose sight of the fact that there's another set of possibilities, one unbound by external obligation and which emerges from a different source: the "coulds." The coulds have always burned inside you, even if you have, until now, remained unaware.

From the Drawing Board. . .to Corporate Boards

Melissa Aubry had been a superstar in private equity. However, the idea of continuing to put in 80- to 100-hour work weeks could not have been more undesirable, given her wish to spend more time with her family. So, her goal became to get on corporate boards, which would generate the income Melissa wanted without taking on the workload that no longer worked for her. She also sought to make the leap from success to significance—and there's a ton of significance and meaning in working on corporate boards.

In our coaching, we started with the basics—creating a resume. Melissa hadn't needed a resume for more than 20 years. She was at such a high level in the field that she didn't even have a LinkedIn profile! So we needed to create a resume that focused not just on her considerable achievements, but also—and this is a key point—the specific needs of the boards she wanted to join.

Most people tend to focus on themselves. Look at everything I've done! But from Aristotle to Dale Carnegie, our greatest teachers have always taught that the key is not how great we are, but how to grasp the needs of the people we want to serve. What are the specific challenges a given company is facing? What deficiencies on the board could Melissa's presence address?

Obviously, we're not going to call out a company and tell them their board is inadequate! Instead, it's about subtly reinforcing the idea that here is an individual with experience and perspective who could be brought in to advise on the specific issues that the target company currently faces. When you go in with that kind of humility, and you focus on the needs of the people you're going to serve, your chances of success are radically higher than if you just talk about your own qualifications.

Once we had done the resume and worked on the interview skills necessary to become a board member (Melissa hadn't had to do a job interview in decades), the work then moved to identifying the right places where she would be interested in serving. We needed to find the people to whom we would reach out and have conversations. We needed to identify those people in Melissa's network who could make introductions to the right people.

You could call it a ground game, just as in politics. Melissa wasn't running for president of the United States. Instead, her goal was to end up on the corporate boards that most fit her interests, experience, and skills. Before long, Melissa was on two boards. The visibility she gained on those boards have made her a natural candidate for additional boards as well.

Melissa's now got the positions she enjoys, the level of income she desires, and the time she needs to enjoy her family. And she doesn't have to work those brutal hours anymore, either.

8

DO WHAT YOU COULD, NOT WHAT YOU SHOULD

So many people drift through life doing what they think they *should* be doing without pausing to ask themselves, "What *could* I do?" This should is so embedded in the fabric of our daily existence that we take it for granted. It's like the air we breathe, ubiquitous but invisible, so we never really question it. But it's the could that strikes a chord with our authentic selves and wakes us up to the fact that the activities that occupy most of our time do not resonate with who we are and what we really want.

The should tends to be externally imposed. It's shaped by the pressure we feel to fulfill certain responsibilities and conform to the expectations of our family, our friends, our peers and colleagues, and society at large. I *should* go to law school because working as an attorney is secure/stable/my friends from college are attending/my parents are lawyers. I *should* accept that promotion at work even though it means a lot more hours and time on the road and I already feel like I'm being squeezed.

The could, in contrast, emerges from within—from our innermost drives, dreams, and desires. And when I say "from within," I mean it literally. When I talk about should versus could with clients and they start thinking about what they would do if they *could* do anything, they often experience a curious physiological sensation, a kind of tingling in the gut. That's your instinct, your authentic self, starting to break out of the layers of duty and commitment (the shoulds) that have suppressed it for so long.

It's as if you're trying to tune in to the radio station of your own soul, but there's another signal (call it Should FM) interfering. When you are able to tune that out and listen to the sweet music of the "could" station unobstructed, you start to understand what has been missing (see Figure 8.1).

Reorienting your worldview from the should to the could shatters the invisible ceiling that limits how you use your time and shape your existence. During the coaching session, this is an exhilarating moment for both client and coach, and I enjoy watching their reaction when they finally consider the possibilities if they removed all risk and obstacles, and if finances or time constraints or family responsibilities weren't an issue. Their face lights up, their voice changes, they sit

Figure 8.1 Move away from the Should and embrace the Could.

up in their chair, alert and attentive. That's the outward manifestation of the inner energy that ignites when they consider the long-buried possibilities and yearnings in their heart. It sounds a little cheesy, but it really happens.

"But Matt," you might be thinking, "that seems appealing, but 'removing all risk and obstacles'? That sounds like the stuff of fantasy. Daydreams won't pay my mortgage."

In this chapter, I'll address that very real objection. My coaching practice is based on dreaming big, *and* is tempered by reality. I don't live in a world of unicorns and rainbows. It's pragmatic and workable. But for now, just approach this as a thought experiment: What could you do if there were no barriers? The should tends to monopolize the conversation and is quick to shout down possibilities with reasons "why not." For a moment, just let the coulds have the floor, unimpeded. We'll see what emerges when they're finally given a chance to speak.

WHY ARE WE SO FULL OF SHOULDS?

One reason the should exerts such power over our lives is because it's usually the path of least resistance, the option that involves less risk and uncertainty; it's more known, better defined. Because it's exogenous, it kind of takes away your agency—you must do X because that's what you're "supposed" to do, and there is a certain levity in removing the burden of choice and letting outside factors "choose for you." But of course there can be a price to be paid for that, and that price can be the deep fulfillment that all of us need to thrive but which remains elusive.

In contrast, aiming for something that we deeply care about, even if it runs counter to the expectations of friends, family, colleagues, and peers, or the norms of society, is riskier. Having a desire, and pursuing that desire, makes us feel more vulnerable. That is the could, which suggests uncertainty. The should implies stability. Choosing this path means that you show yourself, and this exposes you to a greater sensitivity toward the prospect of failure. Of course, the possibility of failing at a should endeavor also exists, but the same vulnerability is not present in the should because you can always rationalize to yourself and others that, "Yeah, I wasn't good at that, but I was never all that interested in it to begin with." It's less emotionally damaging to flub something you're ambivalent about—that you do out of obligation or necessity—rather than something inspired by pure passion, that you really put your heart into or perhaps even see as your life's mission. Think about it—all of the coulds that are hiding in your heart because you have put so much focus on the security of the shoulds! Yet, ignoring our could desires causes pain.

If they go without attention or achievement, you start to really feel it.

I notice that some of my clients who have been tremendously successful in their careers have trouble articulating how they got to where they are. "How could someone achieve so much at something they're not really all that passionate about?" you might wonder. It is a curious phenomenon. I surmise that the qualities that make them high achievers—their intelligence, work ethic, talent, and creativity—compensate for, or disguise the fact, that even as they climbed the ranks in their respective field, it wasn't something they *chose* so much as fell into—something they ended up doing because they felt like they *should*. I have witnessed and worked with a lot of people who had prominent positions but were walking around like zombies—the epitome of "quiet desperation." It really depends on what your definition of success is.

We can also say that there are times when the should is completely appropriate. Quite often, it will align perfectly with what comes from within and what we could do. But it's best when the should and could can line up together. For this to happen, we need to refine our decisions through the internal filtering mechanism (derived from the Why work we do in the Sources/ Drains exercise). That's the only way for a should to make friends with a could. There naturally are areas where the two will go hand in hand.

I believe the predominance of the should emerges in our formative years and especially in the school system, which is based on a regimented study of an established curriculum and a grading system that rewards and incentivizes compliance with that program. In our youth, shoulds are important, as we learn certain life rules, and test how they apply to us. In the school system, and with learning, most of what we study is, obviously, externally imposed. Students learn what the teacher instructs, and teachers follow the curriculum dictated by the school district. You do what you are supposed to do, to get from one level to the next.

Now, that's not necessarily a bad way to educate young minds, but the structured, systematic, top-down nature of education does not leave much room for independent thought or individualized pursuits. Although administrators encourage children to know and use their passions, kids are still there in the system to learn and proceed.

In college and graduate school, we can at least select our area of study and choose our classes from a vast course directory, but by then we've internalized the methodology of instruction. Even at this stage, our educational choices are circumscribed by pressures to learn "marketable" skills in preparation for advancing in the workforce, or for some, by the desire to conform to their parents' vision for their future (especially if the parents are the ones footing the bill).

The popular school structure has us spending so much time thinking and doing (homework, tests, reading), but very little time *seeing*: visualizing our own future. That's the "V" in ACHIEVE," which goes hand in hand with the "C": it must be consequential for you on a deep level. A high school senior may say that she wants to be a journalist or an architect. What will a career in journalism actually look like? What is the lifestyle of an architect, beyond sitting at a computer, considering angles? What's behind the title?

I imagine that for Billy Joel, through all the false starts, early failures, and spirit-crushing setbacks he endured on the road to stardom, he held onto some meaningful image of himself sitting behind a piano on stage at Madison Square Garden, or holding a Grammy in his hand. The visualization of your goal is like your North Star—no matter where you are or how arduous the journey feels, you can always look up and find it shining bright in the sky, a celestial signpost that says, "Don't give up. Keep moving." Your star will prevent you from ever getting lost.

For Billy Joel, working as a self-supporting musician was and is such a long shot (and becoming a bona fide star, a one-in-a-million chance). Following a more stable career would have been the path of least resistance; any occupation holds its challenges, but some definitely involve less risk than others.

But Billy Joel had these tunes in his head, and a calling he could not deny even if he tried. He ignored the should calling his name and kept his mind fixed on the could.

Imagine if he had chosen a different path and ended up doing something else, like becoming an accountant in Newark or a Realtor in Sandusky, instead of a music icon. Suppose "Piano Man" or "For the Longest Time" or "The Entertainer"—the hits you've heard hundreds of times—never even existed? It kind of makes you wonder, to refer back to the lesson of Chapter 5, is the world missing out on your own "Piano Man" because you've given the shoulds all your attention, and ignored the coulds?

DREAM BIG, BUT REALISTICALLY

It's important to note that I'm not dichotomizing shoulds and coulds as "bad" and "good." In fact, many shoulds are positive. We can't, nor will we aspire to, live in a weightless state of unlimited freedom, untethered by responsibilities of any kind. That would not make for a fulfilling experience.

Shoulds exist, but they ought to be compatible with your inner values. When the shoulds overwhelm the coulds, you feel imbalanced, out of whack. A should might be something you do to take steps toward an eventual could, but the point is not to be led by obligations, or to settle when you are hungry for more. It is a common scenario that when we have identified what we could do—what we really want to do—the shoulds should march in. Well, if I am going to run that marathon, I should sit down tonight and map out the week. The should is working in service of the could.

There were definitely times I was living a life heavy with shoulds—I was successful by external accounts, but I still felt unsatisfied. Although I was very involved and active, and even enjoyed working with charity organizations, it wasn't enough to be busy. I wanted meaning. It wasn't until I began working with a coach that I was able to locate the overemphasis on shoulds as the source of my discontent, and to find the solution, to bring a little more could into my life, which in my case was to pursue a career that truly made an impact. I was learning more and more about myself, and really listening. I understood that my energies were coming alive as I worked with my coach, and I was curious to help spark the same kinds of changes in other people. All of my previous shoulds pointed toward my ultimate could: igniting careers and energizing lives for the responding fist pump. This inspires me in a way that none of my other jobs could have ever done.

Again, that's why the C in the ACHIEVE model stands for consequence. The activity has to really matter; there must be meaning for you in this.

But here's the great truth: it's not just about winning the game or being the MVP. Because not everyone is going to be a Billy Joel with an armful of Grammys and millions of adoring fans. Not everyone is going to be Tom Brady hoisting the Lombardi Trophy amidst a rainfall of confetti (again). Emerging on top as "number one" is not the only path to fulfillment; in fact, often, it's a distraction from the true source of happiness.

And ultimately, as you embark on your could path, winning (while something we should aspire to) is not everything, since there is immense value in the attempt itself. I have found that if the goal is meaningful, and one puts in the efforts and takes the right steps, it's okay if it is not fully achieved. There is not a huge sense of loss. Pursuing a meaningful goal, doing all you can, yields a sense of fulfillment and purpose every day.

It could have happened that my attempt at becoming a coach didn't pan out. But I still would have gone through the training and learned new techniques. What would I have done with that learning and experience without a coaching certification? At least then I would have had the qualifications to interview for the kind of corporate job that might truly interest me, maybe a "chief people officer," or a learning and development role. The end result wouldn't be exactly as I had imagined, but it would have been a great step forward. I might have been tapped to go and work with an organization as a senior person in their development group. No matter, following my could would have meant less should in my life and work. And that would have been enough.

As discussed in Chapter 8, my client who was so excited to run the marathon encountered a setback when the whole thing was cancelled. In the face of such trials, we digest this unfortunate turn of events and reimagine the goal, going back to the drivers behind why the goal was chosen in the first place. And then the work focuses on, "What could be done? Given the constraints, what's possible?" The could taps into the deep-rooted feelings, desires, and values, and almost always yields a meaningful alternative—however different from the original goal it may be. As long as you are learning, things are changing. Progressing.

This also speaks to several scenarios I experience with clients. They need their job—it pays the mortgage, private school tuition, etc. But they don't like it. It's not reflective of what they want to do. They may have aspirations of trying a new career—a professional comedian, perhaps. But they are not going to quit their job and take the stage.

Instead, we focus on what it is about being a comedian that activates them. What can they do to scratch that itch that doesn't involve quitting their job? There are improv and comedy classes. Perhaps performing a two-minute set at an open mike night two months from now might be the right step. The client may not realistically be able to pack his bags for a three-month stand-up tour of small clubs, but he can get involved and practice. What does comedy mean to him? How might we bring in some of that alleviation and joy, each week, on a regular basis?

My point is that regardless of your circumstances, there is always some flexibility to modify your life to amplify the presence of the energizing coulds. Sometimes, you don't simply replace your should with a new set of coulds; you find ways to turn the former into the latter, or to discover the could hidden *within* the should.

Though of course as a coach I help people go for their dreams, the practice is still grounded in realism, which often means taking a could and finding a variation of that that is feasible, easy to visualize, and still satisfying—even if it doesn't conform to the definitive ideal. Even if it seems like a moonshot, we can make that goal attainable.

So maybe you're 50 years old and you want to quit your job to take up classical guitar full time. You dabbled in it when you were younger but set it aside when life got in the way, and it's remained a back-burner passion ever since. Now you finally want to give it the time and energy it deserves. Okay. So maybe you won't be playing Carnegie Hall, but what's a variation of that vision that still speaks to you? Perhaps that means playing with a local quartet each weekend, or giving seasonal performances at the local cultural center, or taking lessons with a well-regarded instructor a few hours a week.

Or let's say you aspire to double your sales numbers this year, but the job itself is kind of a drag. Maybe quitting that job isn't the solution. Instead, ask yourself these questions: How can I be creative with this problem? How can I feel empowered and find new sources of satisfaction in your current position? How can I emphasize the positive qualities of your role and minimize the ones that drain your energy?

If love of learning is one of your signature personal strengths, is there a class you can take that will make your job more interesting? If you have the character strength of creativity, is there a new and novel approach you can try? If you're lonely and you want to have a partner, can you find a project to team up with somebody? How can we shine some light into your current life, and develop your gifts?

Perhaps that leads to landing a new position internally, or working with your managers to open a new department where you can apply your underutilized talents more effectively.

And yeah, it sounds nice, the Piano Man and Madison Square Garden and "Matt became a coach and all that." But my methodology is rooted in the reality of family and career, and the limitations of time and space. Sometimes the "could" exercise is not intended to just cast everything aside and start from scratch. More often, it means making the Purpose Puzzle—the elements of your life that exist as they already are—as dark red as possible. And it may take time. It took me 20 years to get here—the culmination of a wide range of experiences and trying different things.

Basically, it's taking some of that should and turning it into a could. That's a key part of goal-setting. Goal-setting doesn't mean indulging in flights of fancy. It means making actionable, ACHIEVE-able plans. After all, the H in the model stands for "hard," not Herculean.

Ultimately, should versus could is not so concerned with rearranging the external circumstances of your life. Rather, it means tapping into your own internal fire to infuse what you do with enthusiasm and spirit. If you feel something, what can you do about it? What's possible? What if I gave that idea some room to breathe and paid it some attention?

THE VOICE OF REASON

Another way of conceiving of the should is thinking of it as a little character who sits on your shoulder (every little character looks creatively different, depending on the individual person) and whispers words of caution into your ear all day long. When he's out of control and hijacks your decision-making, he becomes a tyrant. But that doesn't mean you knock him off his perch and squash him underfoot; it just means you need to rein him in.

That little character is the voice of reason (or maybe you could say voice of caution) that prevents us from making rash decisions and keeps us grounded in reality. He's not an enemy. He's useful, as long as he doesn't crowd out other, more positive, more encouraging voices.

So just as our intention is not to annihilate all the shoulds in our life, neither should we seek to eliminate that little character on our shoulder. Instead, embrace him. He's looking out for you. Just keep him under control.

The voice of reason, as we call it, thinks and acts sensibly. It does not raise eyebrows, put ripples in the water, or buy last-minute airplane tickets to France. There is always a member of every group of friends who holds the role of the voice of reason; she may be very respected for an ability to make calm decisions.

She thinks things through carefully using evidence and logic. However, this reasonable voice might also be quite a spoil sport. She will try to talk you out of any activity that does not make sense to her. She will want to protect you, and judge you, perhaps doing a lot of finger wagging: "I told you so!" But they are a friend, and a valuable one—you just have to find a balance to all of their careful common sense with a healthy dose of emotion and enthusiasm. That little character on your shoulder is kind of like that. Everyone needs a friend to help us think twice. But you probably wouldn't want to hang out with a pack of them. But you do need one good person to be the voice of reason that convinces you not to follow through with some of our "good ideas." No, actually, we shouldn't swan dive off this bridge into the river, even if it looks cool.

One of the great benefits of collaborating with a coach is that the coach can view your situation, your challenges, your problems, and the things that are going well from the outside and help you achieve balance. By virtue of being a trusted, trained, objective, third party, the coach is positioned to get you out of your own head and help make sense of the chorus of voices pulling you in different directions (and all competing to be the loudest voice in the room).

Positive Psychology teaches that we humans have something called a negativity bias no matter how good our lives are. It's a vestige of our evolutionary development that ensured our prehistorical ancestors, who lived a perilous existence full of things that could kill them at any given moment, never let their guard down.

That negativity kept us alert and pushed us forward to improve, prepare, explore, gather resources, and perform whatever other tasks were needed for our survival. No matter how many times we would go outside the cave, we are conditioned to think there might be a bear there waiting for us.

Today, very few people have to worry about being eaten by a bear, but that primal anxiety, written into our DNA, lingers and manifests itself in other, less survival-based ways. As one of my professors shared, the hardware (how we are wired) will take some time to catch up with the software (the inputs and stimuli we experience). Instead of keeping us alert to the mortal hazards of the natural environment, it takes on a different form: "don't get up to that podium because you're going to make a fool of yourself" (the primal fear of being ostracized by the tribe, which would have been fatal to a primitive human who could not survive the hazards of the natural world alone); "don't quit your job to start a business; you'll never succeed" (the primal fear of the unknown combined with the fear of not having enough resources to live).

So even though that voice of self-doubt is coming from a good place, and kept our forebears alive (after all, you and I are here thanks to them, right?), it can prevent us from achieving what we want to achieve. Don't try to squash it; make peace with it. Actually, thank it. Listen to what it's saying while acknowledging that it's one internal voice of many—but don't let it become a tyrant.

INNER MOTIVATION, OUTER MANIFESTATION

The should force is external, whereas the could is what's really in your heart. What you're *driven* to do, rather than what you feel like you *have* to do. Ask yourself both "What should I do?" and "What could I do?" and carefully examine the feelings each question triggers. The former probably elicits a feeling of obligation, maybe a heaviness, a weight. The latter is more likely to stir a sense of pleasure, authenticity, or thrill—a lightness of being, as if an anchor were being lifted from your life.

Taking charge of your future requires an honest appraisal of whether your daily activities are dictated by what you feel you *should* be doing rather than what you *could* be doing. Bringing yourself in alignment with the coulds does not mean eliminating the shoulds entirely, but finding ways to embrace the coulds hidden within or among the shoulds. It's not a black-and-white, binary opposition. Your obligations can coexist with your Piano Man. And you don't need to quit your job or run off to a desert island to make it happen. You can start putting into practice that envisioned life this week, with the right tools and guidance.

Now you're ready to create your own Game Plan that synthesizes all the elements we've talked about over the course of the book.

Constructive Feedback Isn't a Contradiction in Two Terms

A well-known investment management firm had just reached the 10-year mark, and they were at an inflection point in their growth. They were adding lots of people to keep up with the transformation of their business, and they held an off-site to discuss pressing issues facing the company as it grew.

One of the key action items that emerged from the off-site was the need to find a way to get people feedback in a manner that was constructive. They came to me and asked, "How do other companies do it? We are concerned that feedback will devolve into people getting angry and defensive. If that happens, there will be little growth or development We want to do things in a constructive way, and we want to build a culture around the idea that we can attack problems without attacking people."

I did the 360-degree feedback process outlined in this chapter for the top five people in the organization. For each investment professional, I interviewed between 8 and 12 people. I designed an interview guide tailored to the organization and asked the same questions of each person with whom I spoke. This approach helps identify consistencies and inconsistencies. My approach is to try to conduct these interviews in person so I can ask follow-up questions, notice vocal intonation, and go deeper into a question if I sense there is more to share. The more complete the information, the better value we get from the feedback.

I synthesized the information and delivered the feedback report in as constructive and positive a manner as possible.

From there, we parlayed the information into individualized Game Plans. We would then meet regularly to see how they were executing against their plan.

The process worked, and the organization added another six individuals to the executive coaching program. This meant conducting dozens more interviews and creating six more individual Game Plans. Our involvement with the company grew as their success increased. We're now at a point where Inflection Point Partners coaches over 30 individuals at the firm, and they've experienced positive year-over-year results. So, is constructive feedback possible? When you do it the right way, the answer is definitely yes.

9

CREATING YOUR OWN GAME PLAN

Coaching is a collaborative venture, and the creation of the Game Plan reflects that. It's a lot more dynamic and interactive than a one-way process where the client funnels information to me, and I retreat to my office and bang out a draft. We co-create it together. And that co-creation doesn't have to be limited to coach and client. Other people who have a stake in your success, and who benefit when you thrive, can also be involved.

THE GAME PLAN

The Game Plan itself is organized in a grid format. In the left column are five rows: Goal, Vision, Endpoint, Consequences, and Actions. At the top, running horizontally you have three or four goals in separate columns, with their corresponding vision, endpoint, consequences, and actions.

So the whole document is oriented around three or four goals (Figure 9.1). Remember—keep it simple, as a surplus of goals becomes counterproductive. My 2021 Game Plan had four goals: "Quiet the Mind" (daily meditation), "Tools in the Toolbelt" (complete coaching courses and certification exams), "Book It" (get this book done), and "Got Teenagers?" (provide guidance, love, and discipline to protect and connect with my sons).

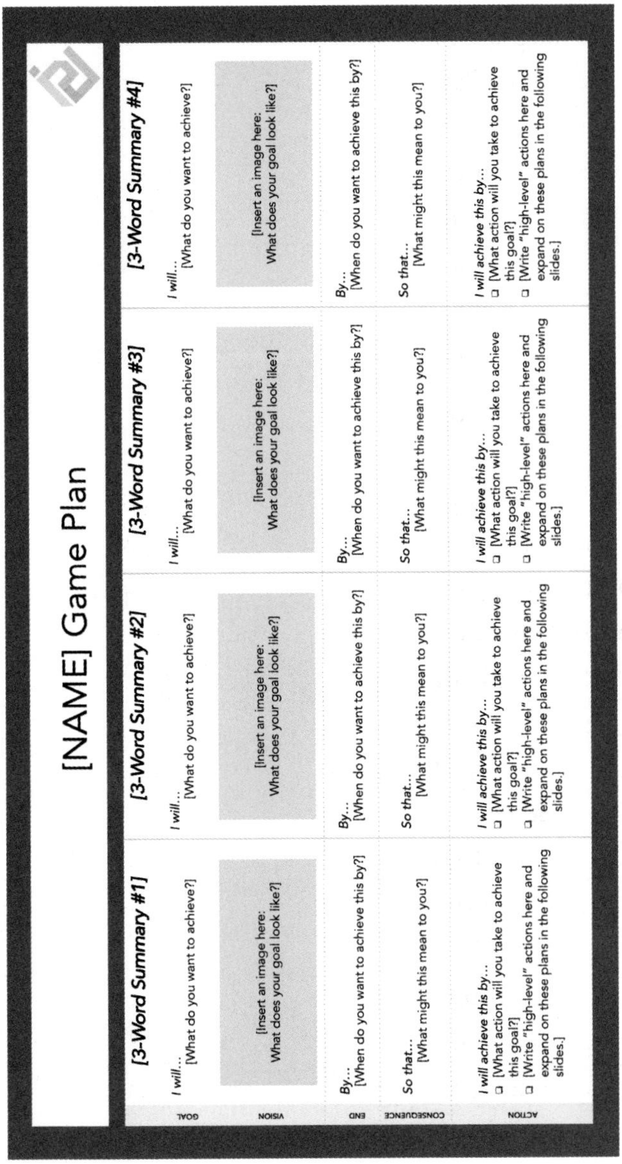

Figure 9.1 A sample Game Plan System.

One powerful technique for juggling multiple goals is *integrating* them. Integrated goals are synergistic because they are correlated in a way that achieving one makes achieving the other more likely. For example, you may have one goal to improve your sleep hygiene and another to compete in a triathlon. Both are dependent on the fitness of body and mind so they kind of exist in tandem, even though they're separate. The more you improve your sleep habits, the better prepared you will be for the grueling training regimen. The more you work out, the likelier it is you'll enjoy deep, restful sleep.

You can see that my 2020 goals are integrated in some ways. Improving my coaching expertise will bolster the book writing process and inform its content, and expanding on my knowledge of meditation and mindfulness will serve all areas of my life.

There's no limit to how many integrated goals you can stack. One client of mine is working on becoming a better communicator, launching a business with his partner, and improving his relationship with his wife and kids. You can imagine how these goals build and feed off each other—it's again that concept of the *gestalt,* wherein the whole is greater than the sum of its parts. Three or four consequential could goals have a powerful cascading effect on one's life. It is better to accomplish a few very focused goals that are thoughtful and come from your heart. You don't need 20.

That said, it's also fine to have nonintegrated goals. Just because a goal doesn't work in tandem with another is not a reason to exclude it. The most important element is that the goals are truly meaningful to you.

The next row on the Game Plan is the vision, a snapshot of the end result. For example, in my own 2020 Game Plan, beneath "Quiet the Mind," I've included a serene image of a picturesque lake, which is emblematic of the state of mind I'm aiming to cultivate. This shows how *anything* can be visualized, even abstract and immaterial goals. The image needs to have meaning to you. What will the goal look like when you achieve it?

Next, a goal should be defined by an endpoint; otherwise, you might never actually get there. Marking the endpoint or the time horizon helps us approach each day with intentionality and conviction. There's no hard-and-fast rule for when to specify the endpoint, which is largely dependent on the goal and the circumstances of the client. If your goal is to run a marathon, then the endpoint will probably coincide with the date of the race. Sometimes we just use the last day of the year to mark the endpoint, for simplicity's sake.

Other endpoints are longer-term or fixed, not by some external circumstance but by your own desire to achieve them within a certain time frame. One client wants to open an overseas office for his business by December 31, 2022, making this a longer-term project. But even if the deadline is far into the future, the act of stating an endpoint helps keep him on track and makes the pursuit of that goal more real. Paradoxically the future goal enables us to focus even more on, and be in, the present. This may strike you as contrary at first, but with closer observation, you will see that committing to a future goal will make you far more mindful of the choices you make and the things you do, right now, in the present. When you are excited for something tomorrow, you'll do everything you can to make it happen, today.

Whatever the endpoint, the idea is that by *visualizing* the conclusion, you can mentally work backwards and demystify the steps required to get from here to there. Stephen Covey, author of *The 7 Habits of Highly Effective People*, touted the importance of "starting with the end in mind," and my system adopts that technique. There is a certain synergy between the visualization and the endpoint setting; they work in tandem, just as integrated goals work synergistically.

The next row on the Game Plan is labeled "Consequence"—the *why* that we've been talking about throughout this book, and the missing link in goal-setting methodologies like SMART. Here, we articulate the purpose and value of each goal. It's critical to have the consequence of each goal printed on the Game Plan itself, which reinforces that the "why" is not

just some nebulous, half-formed idea floating arou..
in your head. It's helpful to be visually reminded of the
purpose driving each goal every time you look at that
chart. In this way, we link the physical pursuit of goals
to immaterial values and strengths that empower us.

Also remember that the why is not something that
we *should* do. The goal needs to come from within,
from the conversation that centers around what you
could do, what has great meaning and heart for you.
Writing and publishing this book allows me to (hopefully) ignite more careers and energize more lives.

Finally, each goal is supported by Actions (see
Figure 9.2) in the bottom row of the Game Plan. These
are concrete steps undertaken to realize each goal. This
is the *how*. The how is the way in which things will
be done to make the what to happen. Again, simpler

Figure 9.2   The ACHIEVE model.

is better; you don't want to overwhelm yourself with too many actions, just as you should keep your daily to-do lists to a minimum. Three to six actions should suffice. Once you begin executing on the plan, these actions become part of your daily routine and rhythm. In the case of a business goal, for example, the goal and the three to six actions listed can be parlayed into a business plan or a strategic plan the leader, team, and company execute together. Try to be as specific or explicit as possible. You need to be able to answer the question, "How am I pacing against my goals?" If you say you will meditate five days a week and you are averaging one, maybe two, this raises the important question "What is getting in the way and what can I do to remove the obstacle?"

DON'T CALL IT A DEVELOPMENT PLAN

For most coaches, their version of the Game Plan is a "development plan," a term that to me feels insipid, uninspired, and austere.

Language matters—how you phrase something influences how it is perceived and, hence, acted upon. *Framing* is the psychological term. And "development plan" is the wrong kind of framing.

That's not to say that the general notion of self-development is wrong—we can all benefit from developing some aspect of our lives—but that development plan tend to speak from a frame of *the need-to-fix problems* rather than *the life-transforming power of maximizing one's strengths*, which is the crux of the Game Plan System. Therein lies the difference.

In my experience, a development plan (much like a "personal improvement plan," another corporate/HR euphemism) becomes, more than anything, a demotivating enumeration of your flaws: here's what you're doing wrong and here's what we think you need to do to fix it. It just harks back to the old, stale version of remedial coaching that served to give underperforming employees a last chance before the company let them go. That is anathema to the Positive Psychology underlying the Game Plan System.

In fact, one of the breakthroughs about Positive Psychology was how it turned the whole field of clinical psychology on its head by eschewing the conventional, pathological approach to human problems (i.e., people are flawed beings with a lifetime of baggage and a litany of neuroses that must be diagnosed and treated) and instead looked at things from a different angle: How can we help people tap into their strengths and virtues to create a life that is happy, fulfilling, and meaningful? Where conventional psychology strives to take people who are living a "happiness deficit" and get them back to neutral, Positive Psychology—and, likewise, my coaching practice—seeks to take people operating at a six or seven, for example, and boost them to the eight or nine they've always thought they could be. Of course, the specific numbers and the scale are less important than the focus on moving people closer to fulfillment, meaning, and satisfaction in their lives.

The Game Plan is built to win. And just as a football team might analyze and practice a hundred plays in the week between last game's final whistle and the next game's kickoff, these are the ones that are going to take us to victory. The Game Plan System concentrates all that mental and physical energy into one succinct, practicable document. I like the idea of the Game Plan just because it creates a sense of energy and excitement and dynamism. After all, goal-setting can be arduous. It involves hard work and that work can be engaging but is sometimes a lot of drudgery. So while "development plan" has uninspiring connotations, the term "Game Plan" reiterates that the process can be fun and energizing.

The client Game Plan is revisited and updated a few times a year (as we regularly refine and upgrade the plan), kind of like the NFL football coach's plan for what needs to be done to win the game on any particular Sunday. It is a very personal document, and it belongs totally to the client.

Currently, I am coaching several individuals within a Private Equity firm and once the plans are done for each, we are going to have a sort of sharing session. Each person will share her Game Plan and will walk the group through her particular goals. The exercise leads to accountability and support, as each person can basically say, "This is what I am working on, and this is how you in this room can be of assistance in helping me accomplish this." Organically, other members of the group reach out and offer resources that might help one another, or offer specific ways to assist. It might be, "I know someone in that department, let me introduce you," or even, "You want to learn to play the guitar? My brother teaches, I will give him a call." Identifying interdependencies is actually one of the greatest things about sharing. It fosters enthusiasm, confidence, and the feeling of not going it alone. Change comes from within, but is made real through the help of others.

THE ROAD SHOW

So, the Game Plan is not just co-created between coach and client/partner—the client may also wish to share it with others. I encourage sharing, as it is the best practice, but I respect that some people choose not to.

Before the plan gets laminated, we "take the show on the road" and share the draft with these stakeholders, which include people at work as well as family (and sometimes others, like personal trainers or fitness coaches, depending on the goals).

Approaching one's co-workers (including the boss) in this fashion is unfamiliar terrain for most people, so I walk them through it and provide some "scripts" to work from, so no one has to wing it.

Typically, the client will say, "As you may know, I've partnered with an executive coach ("partnered" is the key word; I try to avoid using the verb "work") and I want to share my Game Plan with you." This gives the clients the opportunity to explain to their team what matters to them, what they're working toward, what they're passionate about, and how those individuals can play a role in the pursuit of the client's goals (which will also impact divisional and corporate goals).

The "road show" facilitates accountability by bringing the Game Plan to light (making it a public project rather than just a private initiative) and opening the door to feedback and support from others. After all, most goals are not created and pursued in solitude. Individual goals tend to revolve around development of the self, but in a way that is intertwined with other people. Individual goal-setting relies on social execution, you might say.[1]

---

[1] Klein, H.J., Lount Jr., R.B., Park, H.M., and Linford, B.J. (2020). When goals are known: the effects of audience relative status on goal commitment and performance. *Journal of Applied Psychology* 105 (4), 372–389. https://doi.org/10.1037/apl0000441.

This social aspect is especially evident when it comes to improving your management skills, or reconnecting and deepening the bonds with your family—which happen to be two of the most common goals I coach people on.

Just the act of humbly and openly approaching your stakeholders, be they your boss, your peers, or your subordinates, in a spirit of self-improvement will greatly enhance your stature in their eyes. They'll be impressed that the 360 interviews they took part in are actually being listened to and addressed (how many corporate surveys and questionnaires have you filled out, only to never hear anything about them again?). It's refreshing for people to know that someone is actually listening and taking their input to heart. And this can be the first step toward building new relationships and strengthening existing ones.

You'll then explain to them the broad strokes of your Game Plan and that you're open to additional feedback in the months to come as you work to implement the plan, emphasizing that the stakeholder's input and engagement remains a vital part of the ongoing process (not just in the diagnostic phase).

Of course, this is all done through the lens of positivity: not fixing problems but growing, learning, and improving in a way that enhances not only you but everyone in your orbit. People will admire and respect you for this.

BACK-AND-FORTH PROCESS

At this stage, the client and I haven't yet created the final Game Plan version that gets laminated and hung proudly on the wall. Based on conversations with other stakeholders and with me, the client has the option to make additional changes. The co-creation process usually involves two to three iterations of the document where the client and I pass it back and forth, tweaking and refining it until it's ready.

The ACHIEVE model is a useful rubric during this phase, too, because many of my suggestions and questions serve to make sure the elements of ACHIEVE are upheld and in balance with one another. For example, clients tend to articulate goals initially that are vague. The first "E" in ACHIEVE is *explicit*, so often I challenge them to chip away some more of the marble to bring out the smoother, flawless finished form, and articulate goals that are clear and succinct. The key question will always be how you are making progress, in terms of the written Game Plan. A very specific goal might be that you want to lose 15 pounds. We will write out exacting actions to help meet that goal (going to the gym for 45 minutes five times a week, walking for one hour every day, seeing a nutritionist twice per month). And if the goal is vague ("I want to travel more"), we create definite, precise steps and actions to make this goal attainable (schedule time off from work, take day excursions every month, plan trips with family and friends). I do not judge a client's goals—I just help make them happen. We will know our progress by what we do on a day-to-day basis.

Another common mistake is length—sometimes they'll write three pages worth of Game Plan material. But more is not necessarily better—sometimes, it's just more. On the contrary, often, a measure of an idea's strength—be it a book idea, a business plan, a community service project, or a mathematical formula—is that it can be succinctly, elegantly described. After all, the plan's purpose is to generate action. We don't want to be distracted by too many words. Verboseness and/or over-complexity is usually a sign that the plan or goal is too vague, or that it is unworkable. Less is more. The measure of an idea's strength, rather than its length, is what we focus on.

When the Game Plan is finalized after several rounds of feedback and revision, the goals, vision, endpoint, consequences, and actions (by targeting things within your control) will be in sync—making you into a well-oiled, goal-achieving machine—with every element moving together in balance.

Now, finally, we're reaching a point where we can execute, which entails assessing results, problem-solving obstacles, celebrating wins, and setting new goals as you charge forward confidently toward the realization of your life's mission.

The HALO Effect

Pete Moore is one of those brilliant business guys who seemingly can crank out a new idea every minute of the business day. He sleeps with a pad of paper or a phone by his bed, so he can capture more ideas in the middle of the night. Pete is the CEO of Integrity Square, a financial advisory and early-stage growth equity firm that specializes in the Health & Wellness sector.

It's fantastic to have the ability to come up with so many brilliant ideas. It can also pose a challenge, however, when determining which of the 20 to 30 ideas you have are viable. That was the challenge he faced when we got together. As I told Pete, we only have a finite amount of time and energy each day. And the team needs to focus on what's most important.

We conducted a 360-degree feedback process. I gathered information from Pete's entire leadership team, including investors and others across the organization. I also administered personality and character trait assessments. We sat to discuss the synthesized information feedback report.

Based on the report, we co-created a Game Plan. This document, which housed Pete's four most important and consequential goals, provided the guardrails Pete needed to funnel his energy and creativity. During the process, Pete originated a practice I now use with many of my clients by asking himself daily: To register a "W" (representing a Win) for today, what are the three things I will have started, completed, or continued? (Recognizing we don't always complete things in a day.) Pete noticed it wasn't 20 things. Or even 10. Three, sometimes four, well thought-out actions can yield the desired outcomes for that day.

As we gained more focus, Pete felt that the "Wellness" in Health & Wellness fell far short of what the sector should represent. So, Pete and his team trademarked a new term around which they fortified their entire business: HALO—Health, Active, Lifestyle, Outdoor. Pete launched a successful podcast called HALO Talks. He also created an education series called HALO Academy. Pete and his team now sit at the center of this newly renamed HALO sector.

Pete's a charismatic guy. He's gregarious. He lights up a room. And now Pete's got the focus he wanted, allowing Integrity Square to be the dominant, go-to firm for any serious player in the Health & Wellness sector—make that HALO sector—who wants to raise real money. And now the HALO term has become the equivalent of a Good Housekeeping Seal of Approval of companies in Pete's space. That's the power of focus.

10

EXECUTING THE GAME PLAN: CELEBRATING WINS, HANDLING SETBACKS, ACHIEVING GOALS, AND CREATING NEW ONES

Until now, we've mostly been talking about the prep work involved in developing the Game Plan—everything that leads up to the moment when the printed sheet takes a victory lap through the lamination machine. That we've talked so much about planning and not so much about execution is a reflection of the "go slow to go fast" mantra—the more you invest up front, the smoother the process will be once you launch. As Abraham Lincoln is reputed to have said, "Give me six hours to chop down a tree, and I'll spend the first four sharpening the axe." Einstein had a similar mantra: "If I had an hour to solve a problem, I'd spend 55 minutes thinking about the problem and 5 minutes thinking about solutions."

Now we're at the point where coach and client put the plan into action. Execution, of course, brings its own set of challenges. Consequently, we set a regular cadence of meeting times to assess progress and figure out what changes can be made to bolster your efforts at reaching your Game Plan goals. The discussion is usually centered around three questions: What's going well? What's getting in the way (the friction points)? What will we have accomplished by next week?

These questions allow the necessary self-scrutiny to address shortcomings while maintaining the positive psychological framework of emphasizing strengths and celebrating accomplishments.

CHANGE IS SCARY

The task of figuring out the why, what, and how that will lead you out of a life of quiet desperation can be challenging. Looking inside yourself and asking weighty, existential questions about who you are and what you truly want from your time here on earth forces you to venture intellectually and emotionally outside of your comfort zone.

But putting the Game Plan into practice means turning thought into action, and that can be especially scary because it's a different kind of departure from one's comfort zone, one that frequently necessitates some kind of behavioral change. It's one thing to imagine a change, quite another to do it.

Humans tend to thrive on structure, order, and routine—of course, we also have a natural predilection for novelty, but in limited doses. Our innate sense of caution (which again is closely linked to that evolutionary fear of what will happen if we wander outside the cave) leaves us with a feeling of trepidation when we have to alter our habits. But fear is normal, and a coach will stand beside you and support you as you make those changes.

Remember that finding your Piano Man and building your life around the could, rather than the should, often entails abandoning the path of least resistance for a much more uncertain one. The familiar is comforting and safe; the unfamiliar can be anxiety-inducing and disorienting. But it can also be exhilarating, inspiring, and rewarding in a way that playing it safe is not. In time, the fear subsides, and the positive effects become more pronounced.

It's a long journey, and you will struggle with it at times. On days when that "What the hell am I doing?" anxiety clouds your vision or assaults your positive attitude, or when self-doubt ("I'm not good enough to achieve all this") rears its ugly head, simply turn back to your Game Plan itself. That's the anchor that keeps your boat moored securely when stormy weather knocks you around. (Recall the dual meaning of the acronym GPS: boaters also rely on their GPS to navigate safely.) Without that Game Plan, the frenetic wind of real life will blow your boat around in circles. You may cover some ground, but you won't get anywhere.

Remind yourself why you're undertaking this pursuit, what it means to you, and what it will take to cross the finish line. Those who have a *why* to live, as Viktor Frankl said, can bear with almost any *how*. Focus on the images printed on the placard that represent the endpoint and what achieving that goal would mean to you. Consequence plus visualization: this will be the source of your tenacity as you fight your way to the top.

It's also important to dispel the notion that experiencing anxiety is somehow a sign that you're not good enough, that it's indicative of being underqualified for a task, and that the best and brightest coast through change with a cool, unswerving confidence.

After coaching numerous high-performing individuals—people who are veritable stars in their field—I can attest that this notion is false. The "winners" whom you may admire are perhaps good at masking their own fear, but self-doubt and success certainly coexist. There is something a little counterintuitive about this, but it's a fact. It's more about how they use these emotions. Instead of letting these feelings block them, they do what they can to use it as fuel to propel them. "How can we use these feelings to move you forward?" is one of the questions that comes up in our coaching sessions.

Nor does that anxiety necessarily disappear once you pass a certain career threshold or rack up X number of accolades. Instead, what happens as you rise through the ranks is that each promotion brings with it a new set of challenges, skills, and responsibilities. The stakes get bigger; the cost of failure is amplified. And often, the higher you climb the ladder, the farther you tend to drift from the particular specialization or skillset that made you so "promotable" in the first place. So with more professional accolades, more prestige, more money, and more influence come new sources of self-doubt.

I have one client in the tech industry who has vaulted into a C-level executive position after a few fast promotions through upper management. But he started as a technician—he excelled at software engineering, not leading teams. And even as he ascended the corporate hierarchy, he received little in the way of formal training or education in management. He has worked hard to do well in each new position, but he has always felt like he was just barely holding on, staying one mere step ahead of everything imploding. He has the impostor syndrome, in other words.

A few months ago, in one of the first big "tests" in his new executive role, he had to lead an all-hands meeting involving several hundred employees (the first gathering of its kind in the company's history). The stakes were high.

To prepare for this particular test, we collaborated on a script (he wrote it; I advised) that he practiced with me, a hypothetical audience member, which allowed him to cultivate the confidence needed to deliver the big speech. By doing this role play, he visualized his success—more than visualized, in fact. He simulated it. He was energized. And it worked.

He was always capable. He just had to make friends with the fear of the unknown. As he continues advancing on his Game Plan, many of our coaching sessions have concentrated on empowering him to handle this *terra incognita* with confidence. After all, athletes have been tapping into the power of visualization for decades. Why can't we do the same thing?

I've encountered similar crises of confidence throughout my own career, when I was thrust into a position of prestige which, instead of feeling proud and satisfied for the achievement, just made me wonder if I was even worthy. I wrote earlier of my sophomore baseball debacle, when I couldn't handle the spotlight, and one mistake begat another—a cascading spiral of pessimism and failure. Within weeks I had plummeted from the heights of being the youngest starting shortstop in the league to self-sabotaging game after game, until the coach had no choice but to bench me.

Eventually, I earned back the starting role and in my final two years distinguished myself as an excellent player, collecting a number of awards in the process. But it had less to do with my physical ability. My arm wasn't as strong post-surgery, but my positive mental attitude helped me to compensate as I gained my post-surgery force back. I was able to bounce back by shaking off the negativity and focusing instead on a clear *vision* of what success looked like.

For clients who are struggling with the change process, I reacquaint them with the power of visualization. Where are you now, and where do you see yourself at the end? See yourself there, doing what you want to do and feeling how you want to feel. Let that vision burn bright in your mind—that's the guiding light that leads you out of the darkness.

If your goal is moving to a new city, but you're struggling to uproot yourself from the ties that bind you in your current location, your image might be the view of the leafy, picturesque street outside your window in the comfortable apartment where you'll make your new home. If you're working hard to lose weight, and the fridge is beckoning you from across the room, you squash that temptation by visualizing six-pack abs. If your goal is to reconnect with your family, you might imagine dancing with your wife or kids at your daughter's bat mitzvah.

These visions link the present state with the future destination; they connect inner desire to exterior circumstances. And what is goal achievement but the process of shaping external reality to harmonize with an inner wish? Seeing really is believing—in yourself. An effective coach meets you where you are and helps you uncover your vision, then empowers you to get there.

Of course, visualizing success of your goal is motivated by the importance of the goal itself: being "consequential." The "C" and the "V" in the ACHIEVE model have a certain symbiosis—they strengthen and reinforce each other. Visualization makes a goal (even a lofty, difficult, or distant one) more accessible, concrete, and real. And a meaningful goal elicits powerful motivation from within you, one that translates into a sharper, more vivid image of the endpoint.

WHY SOME CLIENTS STUMBLE WHILE OTHERS STAY THE COURSE

Fear and anxiety generated by venturing outside one's comfort zone (and into the unknown) are, as I said, normal. They're not "problems" per se; just natural challenges that come with carving out your own path. Change of any sort causes an internal reaction. Just don't judge it—know that anxiety means things are happening.

A lack of enthusiasm for working with a coach can be a problem, because coaching only works if you're genuinely committed to the process. Sometimes, clients do not reach out to me of their own volition but rather at the urging of a spouse (or perhaps a boss or a friend). Maybe this is just a much-needed kick in the pants that wakes them up to the fact that coaching is, despite their initial skepticism or disinterest, exactly what they need. But if a client is just going through the motions to please someone else, the partnership may not work out. Someone might contact me and say, "Matt, my wife would really benefit from working with you," and leave contact information. My reply would be, "Thank you for reaching out, please have her contact me." I would not send an email to introduce myself to the individual, because the desire, the motivation, the goals, and the work have to be hers. Obviously, given that my whole practice is based on finding what deeply resonates with *you* and restructuring your life around what you *could* do rather than what you *should*, if coaching itself is just another *should* imposed externally, it's not going to fare well.

This same principle applies when I engage with organizations. When companies hire me, I advise that they *don't* make the engagement mandatory for their executives. The partnership thrives when all parties are present because of a strong desire to be there, not because it's another obligation mandated from above.

Sometimes, the client stumbles when their initial enthusiasm burns bright but fades as time goes on. Warning signs of flagging interest include when clients repeatedly cancel appointments or when they routinely fail to do their "homework." It's best to come to each session fully present and engaged. However, as many of my clients are high-performing professionals, I understand that scheduling for meetings is not always simple. In this case, I encourage a short call, even five minutes, that allows for a bit of space to think and reflect. Even the briefest check-in will reaffirm one's commitment to their Game Plan. I like to think of this short call as breathing space; by the time they hang up the phone, they have a little bit more energy and a little bit more direction. They might even feel physical relief. I like to say that if you are really busy, let's make sure it is good busy—and that you know what you are doing and where you are going. Carving out space will keep you focused and animated.

I can tell when clients are distracted, but I don't berate them for it; I try to use that distraction as a jumping off point for discourse: "Joe, I'm getting the sense you have some things on your mind. What's going on?" It's a way of challenging the client's apparent absent-mindedness in a nonconfrontational way that leads to productive exploration about whatever is really bothering him.

If a client relegates coaching to the back burner, it's not necessarily because of lack of interest, but simply because she is overextended. Crises at the office and obligations at home may take precedence over other things. And having a coach may *seem* like a luxury, while keeping your job and maintaining a stable family life are indispensable.

But these things are not mutually exclusive, and actually, the periods when you're feeling overwhelmed and "just don't have time for a session this week" are an ideal time to connect, and lean on me for help. A single coaching call or meeting will be the jolt of clarity that you need. As well, why are you so busy? What has you feeling overwhelmed? A coaching call or session will reconnect you with your priorities and your true purpose. That's what I'm here for—to enable you to pursue what's most valuable to you even when other factors are greedily gobbling up your attention, time, and energy! Slowing down to go fast often makes the most sense and is the best path forward.

You don't want to isolate yourself when things become difficult. Draw on the assistance of your coach, while also tapping into the strength and support of your inner circle—the stakeholders with whom you shared your Game Plan or who were involved in the diagnostic process. Utilize their expertise and their desire to help you (and, I assure you, they *do* want to help).

In any case, if clients feel like they're spinning their wheels, it's usually helpful to shift the discussion from the *how* (the action steps the client is taking, or not taking, as the case may be) back to the *why*. We return to the introspective drawing board that initiated the whole goal-setting process and revisit the drive and purpose behind your goals. Why might this matter, and if you were to accomplish this, how will it positively impact you? Answering these questions provides clarity to the process if your vision and dedication have become fuzzy or unfocused.

STAY POSITIVE, AND REMEMBER YOUR STRENGTHS

One of the pillars of Positive Psychology is that well-being depends in part on organizing your life around your existing strengths. If you're experiencing difficulty executing your Game Plan, you don't need to come up with a new set of tools to deal with it. You already have everything you need.

If a client says, "Matt, I don't know what steps to take next. This is much harder than I expected," we return to the strengths and values inventory, and discuss how to utilize them so as to power through whatever obstacles are in the way.

Last year I worked with a client who relocated to Japan to head the establishment of an overseas division with her company, a once-in-a-lifetime opportunity that fulfilled two long-term goals of hers: to live in Asia and to be promoted to an elite tier of upper management. Finally, she felt like she had been given the chance to put her many talents to use. But the expansion into the Japanese market was a rocky road, full of unexpected setbacks and seemingly interminable crises. Combined with the stress of adapting to a new country and culture, her dreamed-of opportunity started seeming like an unhappy slog.

"I'm feeling like I really don't even want to be here. I'm not enjoying this at all," she confessed during a session.

My response was to flip the negative framing on its head and instead of focusing on what she *didn't* like, examine the problem through the lens of what she *did*. We switched up the conversation to talk about what she *was* doing well, with self-confidence. That's Positive Psychology in practice.

The negativity bias that all of us carry within us can overshadow our natural abilities, preventing us from appreciating our existing talents and making us perceive the current situation as bleaker than it actually is. Slow down, step back, and look at things through a more generous perspective. This, of course, is easier said than done, but that's another benefit of working with a coach: it's someone who can help "get you out of your own head."

CELEBRATE WINS

Pursuing goals is a long highway. Some goals stretch on for years. For long-term initiatives (and shorter ones, too), it's easy to get lost in the day-to-day grind, or feel like you're not making substantial progress.

Therefore, as the coaching engagement unfolds, I make it a point to celebrate wins—the small moments of triumph that eventually add up to a big victory at the end. These celebrations provide vital bursts of motivation and remind you of your forward motion, even if it seems on the surface like you're advancing at a glacial pace.

In a similar vein, in lieu of fretting over when that final, culminating accomplishment is going to come, I urge my clients to simply strive to "win the day." Winning the day means, "Have you made progress, however incremental? Were you able to check off the two or three things on your to-do list in pursuit of that objective?" You did what you could, for that goal, on that particular day.

A good practice is to write out three things that you have either started, continued, or completed that will make today a win (W). Of course, most activity will fall into the continued category, as we don't start or complete goals and big tasks on a daily basis.

Then you can write a W on the calendar. It's that simple.

Keep that overarching goal in mind, but don't get overwhelmed by the fact that it's distant and there's a lot of bumpy real estate separating you from your current position to your desired one. As I stated earlier, focusing on future goals enables us to be more present; although it may seem paradoxical, knowing where you want to go makes you very mindful in what you do during the present day.

Win the day is also an effective fear mitigation technique because it reinforces the idea that you're not going to achieve some momentous milestone every single week. That would be a narrow, and ultimately misguided, definition of success. Success is not the grand, climactic fireworks-and-confetti moment of achievement; instead, it's constituted by the small, unsung, minor victories along the way. It's not the instant you plant your flag on the summit; it's each and every step that carried you on the path to the top.

THE ROAD IS BETTER: COMPLETING GOALS AND CREATING NEW ONES

While realizing goals is exciting, it can also be anticlimactic. One of life's little ironies is that the journey is usually more satisfying than the destination, or, as Cervantes put it, the road is better than the inn. It is the feeling you have when working toward your destination that gives the day-to-day meaning and purpose. If you've arrived, what is left?

This seems counterintuitive, especially when "the road" can be so arduous, and even punishing. What accounts for this curious fact? Well, the high that comes when you ascend the podium to have the gold medal (proverbial or otherwise) draped around your neck is fleeting—a burst of exhilaration that fades quickly and is frequently followed by a feeling of "that was fun, but now what?" The hard work it took to get to that point may have been painful, but there is a certain pleasure in that pain, when it's endured in service of something that is (that magic word again) *consequential*. Moreover, we learn and improve from that pain. The road sharpens our skills, tests our mettle, and strengthens our character and discipline. There is immense satisfaction in that process.

Humans thrive on structure, but we enjoy being challenged and staying active. I'd say that's doubly true of high-performing individuals. People do well when we have a project that tests their mental and physical stamina, and keeps them engaged. That, too, is evolutionary in origin—the earliest humans, our distant ancestors, survived their brutish prehistoric reality thanks to ceaseless toil against scarcity and threat. They were, by necessity, workers, strivers, doers, rarely at rest. Their lives depended on it. Today, of course, there's less selection pressure, and more room for indolence and hedonism and just resting on our laurels. But the default human condition is to want to stay busy, to be engaged, and to learn, and to build on our previous successes by achieving something even more meaningful.

When I was training for my first New York City Marathon, I daydreamed about the moment when I would cross the finish line—the very thought was pleasurable. I yearned for that ecstatic feeling of triumph. But when it actually happened, it didn't pack the euphoric punch I expected.

After some reflection, I realized that it wasn't *completing* the goal that really made me happy but everything that led up to it: the rigorous mental and physical preparation, the camaraderie I enjoyed with friends (I trained and ran with my dear friend, Chris Schmidt, a lieutenant in the NYC police department) who were involved, and of course the race itself: huffing and puffing through the five boroughs. But the gratification had little to do with the finish line—and certainly not with "winning" anything.

When you do finally achieve your goals, take time to reflect on what it meant from you and what you gained. You will likely discover that the real value lay in the hard work, and not the payoff.

And now that it's over, you will probably feel motivated to establish new goals. There's never really a point in life when we say, "Well, that's it—I've set out to do everything I've ever wanted. What's good on Hulu these days?" Rest, relax, and enjoy the feeling of getting it done before rushing into the next project, but it's natural to want to do more, learn more, climb the next hill, and slay the next dragon. Stasis is anathema to the human spirit.

And that means creating new goals.

In some cases the new goal simply becomes *maintaining* the accomplishment of the previous one. This is especially true of fitness goals; for example, you set out to lower your body fat to 12%, but now you must transition into the next phase of that project, which is staying lean and trim (a challenge unto itself).

Besides maintaining, how does one develop new goals? By returning to the same methodology we used before. Fortunately, we've already gone through the introspective rigor of finding your Piano Man, which is an eternal wellspring of inspiration and motivation. What else can you do in fulfillment of that which has value to you and which resonates with your strengths?

Essentially, when executing a Game Plan, as a former MTV colleague of mine said, we're always in beta—never standing still. We are always reflecting, tweaking, improving, and moving forward. When you feel anxious, embrace that anxiety as a normal and even healthy response to the unknown, as long as you mitigate it by staying the course, counting on the support of your coach and other stakeholders, and maintaining the focus on your strengths (what you *can* do rather than what you can't, and what you *really want* to do). And at every point, reflect on the *why*. It's easy to overlook the all-encompassing reason behind all of this, especially as you get busy, frustrated, or consumed by day-to-day action steps.

There are many moving parts to the Game Plan System. The *why* is what ties it all together. The why is you. The what is that which you produce. Tie it tight enough, and you'll be able to hold fast until the end.

The road to fulfilling a purpose-driven life is paved with meaningful goals in increments, one after another.

Figure 10.1   How to ACHIEVE™.

The GPS will guide you to and through them. I summarize my approach to achievement with the key phrases in Figure 10.1.

If you'd like to see examples of Game Plan Systems I've created for my clients, please visit my website inflectionpointpartnersllc.com.

Getting Your Team to Think Bigger

How do you get an organization that's doing just fine to think bigger and act bigger? After all, you can only coast one way. . .downhill, right? This was the challenge facing my client Gwen Sidely, a successful real estate CEO. Her firm had been buying up multi-family homes and wanted to move up to buying apartment buildings in high-end communities. Yet her team of 20 resisted the idea of making such a bold move—after all, things are going just fine, so why rock the boat?

During our work together incorporating my Game Plan System, Gwen realized that to take on the growing demands of incoming business opportunities, including investing in and partnering on radically larger projects, the organization needed to shift its mentality to a higher level. Her team was capable of making the move. They just didn't believe they could, or that there was value in taking on more growth (and more risk).

Gwen and I strategized together, trying to find the best approach to pushing the organization forward. One idea we hit on was to create and place laminated Game Plans in the hand of every employee. This meant that not only the management but also every staff member would know what to work toward on any given day. We moved forward with the plan, and found that it injected a spirit of focus and growth into the whole company.

But that wasn't the only benefit. The Game Plans also paved the way for more substantive reviews and feedback sessions. Once we defined the company's expectations of each employee and knew each staff member's goals, Gwen and the managers were much better equipped to discuss performance.

Working together, we took the opportunity to strengthen staff members' commitment to the overall vision and direction of the company as well. We included language related to the mission, vision, and values on the Game Plans, discussed these ideas regularly in meetings, and featured them prominently at an off-site session I led at the annual retreat. The most recent retreat was titled Next Level. And the company was now partnering on deals that just a short while ago would have been out of reach.

11

LET'S CONTINUE THE CONVERSATION

There's a wealth of information out there about how to live the life you've imagined, and many professionals with various credentials and honorifics appended to their name who are eager to dispense advice on how to do it. Unfortunately, much of that information is misguided, and many of those professionals, while acting in good faith, will supply you with bad ideas and ineffectual methods.

So it's no wonder that so many people still lack much-needed direction in key areas of their life—even when they're very accomplished in others. No wonder so many wrestle with the feeling that something important is still missing despite all they've achieved, and all that's going well. There's a feeling that the jigsaw puzzle of their existence is half-finished, and the cover art on the box remains obscured and incomplete.

Worse, perhaps, than the prevalence of this feeling among successful ambitious people —a vague sense of lacking at best and a "quiet desperation" at worst—is the fact that they often feel that they're alone in the experience. They blame themselves for feeling this way. I'm here to reassure you, both as a coach drawing on a wealth of experience and an individual whose own road has been meandering and full of detours, *you aren't alone*. Moreover, the blame does not lie with you.

My mission is to ignite careers and energize lives. My fuel is to see the fist pump, or whatever version of that is for you. In some instances, my partnership helps jolt people out of inertia by guiding them to the discovery of an alternative path, one that resonates with their true self and reorients their life around activities of great personal *consequence.*

Consequence is the missing link that inhibits so many of us. Missing is perhaps a misnomer. It isn't absent—it's just hidden, requiring work (often partnering with a coach) to bring it into the daylight. That act of discovery, when it happens to you, will mark one of the great inflection points of your trajectory. The picture on the puzzle box finally starts to take shape, and the things you've been working on, or toward, finally begin to coalesce into a meaningful whole.

Everything originates from that consequence, that purpose—the *why*. Without it, it's difficult to develop and pursue any kind of long-term plan, whether at work, at home, or at play. Once you unveil the *why* within you, the *what* and the *how* become clearer, as well.

In structural engineering, as in nature, one of the strongest shapes with which to build a complex system is the triangle, and the symbiotic trio of the why/what/how demonstrates that dynamic, too: three parts that strengthen each other and hold each other together.

One of the significant shortcomings of SMART goals and other goal-setting practices is that they don't encourage sufficient introspection about the *why*, rendering them inert—powerless. Purpose is the electrical charge that courses through the action steps you take to turn a vision into a reality. You need that electricity to keep you moving forward. When I talk about energy, I mean your meaning, passion, and significance, and how it is expressed through your voice and your body. Your energy goes in the direction of your purpose, and following that charge of energy is the best advice I can give to somebody.

The journey is often a difficult one, but that very difficulty can be a potent source of energy and inspiration. Bringing one's inherent strengths to bear against a formidable obstacle sharpens our skills, fortifies our spirit, amplifies our confidence, and delivers a deeper, more sustainable sense of fulfillment than just lounging on easy street. There is something paradoxical in this notion, especially in a culture where pleasure is often equated with happiness, but as anyone who has achieved something requiring intense, sustained effort and vast intellectual and emotional labor will attest, it's true. Grit, sacrifice, and hard work aren't simply the price one pays for the prize. They *are* the prize. In the same way, muscle grows and is strengthened when placed under duress and pressure.

Therefore, we should embrace the challenges that show themselves as we execute our own Game Plan, and embrace the ambiguity that surrounds the pursuit of our goals. We can accept the fact that the journey, by nature, is characterized by uncertainty. Every road is marked by twists and turns, and even if you *do* end up where you first expected, it's often by a different route than the one you mapped out when you started. The self-discovery and sharpening of one's personal, social, mental, and emotional strengths that results from this process is one of the great benefits of a coaching engagement. Ultimately, the road is better than the inn.

And remember that "the road" doesn't have to be a remote highway in Tanzania or a winding mountain track around the Andes—it may just be a few towns over. By that I mean that the Game Plan System is not exclusively a methodology for completely redesigning your life. Among the individuals I work with, that kind of top-to-bottom self-reimagining is the exception. For each client who comes to me in search of a 180-degree change, there are five who are just looking for guidance on how to thrive in their current role and learn new skills to stay the course. Coaching isn't always a gut renovation of the entire house. Sometimes it's just a kitchen remodel or a fresh coat of paint—an understanding of what's driving you and how you might be perceiving and viewing your day-to-day.

In the same vein, setting a goal does not mean you will land on the moon. It does not have to be sensational or grandiose to be worthwhile. While I do coach people who are chasing after lofty, staggering objectives, most goals are a little more down to earth. The merit of a goal has less to do with its prestige than with its congruence with your values, desires, and vision. Your goal might be to be elected to the Senate. Your goal might be to jump from the high diving board at the local pool. Whatever it is, you can do it.

Earlier, I spoke of the distinction between the could and the should, and goal-setting is another terrain where the coulds and the shoulds in your life jockey for power. Are your daily activities dictated by obligation, by external pressure, by things you *should* do? Or is there a healthy balance between the shoulds and those activities you *could* do if you were unfettered by the limitations of time, space, money, and family? How might you view or reframe shoulds as coulds?

These are questions that seem so elementary when written on paper, and yet they remain elusive to most people. Even though they strike at fundamental truths like, "What do I want to do with my life? How do I want to spend my time? Why am I not doing it?" they fade into the white noise of quotidian existence, or are consigned to that perpetual thing we will do when we "have the time." Life is too short to keep growing that existential junk drawer of dreams put on hold.

Hence, when it comes to figuring out their purpose, most people are not only *not* getting the right answers, they're also rarely even asking the right questions. One evening, working late, they may look up from the glow of their laptop, turning their attention away for a moment from the ceaseless stream of emails, meetings, obligations, and tasks. Maybe the photo-of-the-month on the wall calendar will catch their eye, and they'll take a deep breath. Perhaps it's a pristine tropical beach, or a snowy countryside hill—some visualization that makes them acutely aware of some deeper, untapped longing. And the date on the calendar tells them that another year has gone by, a year of thousands of hours of work with no discernible progress toward that elusive sense of inner desire that remains, so it seems, just out of reach.

Fortunately, there's plenty of space in life for change and growth, and room on that office wall for your Game Plan. If not, it's probably time to ask for a bigger office—you can take that literally or metaphorically. The GPS is the manifestation, the synthesis of all the component parts of ACHIEVE – **actionable steps, consequence**, goals that are **hard** (yet realistic), **integrated**, and **explicit**, and **visualization**, capped off by an **endpoint** that will keep you on track by establishing a linkage and a connection to the process.

As coaches, we foster transformative partnerships between ourselves and the client. Transformative is the key word, as one of the critical outcomes involves closing the gap between where the client begins the process and what the client wants to work toward. So, when we ask, "What is possible?" we have the most effective method of capturing the desired destination and determining the means to get there. We have a process. It is a reflective methodology that involves holding a mirror up to the client's reality in a way that lets her discover her own truth and part the tangle of branches impeding her true path.

What's possible? Nearly anything. You can do it— but you certainly do not have to go it alone.

It's time to fit the puzzle of your life together.

"You can be anything you want to be, if only you believe with sufficient conviction and act in accordance with your faith; for whatever the mind can conceive and believe, it can achieve."

– Napoleon Hill

So, what do you really want to Achieve?

ABOUT THE WEBSITE

This book is accompanied by a website:
www.inflectionpointpartnersllc.com/book
The website includes:

- Game Plan Template
- Example Game Plan
- Purpose Puzzle
- ACHIEVE Model
- Sources/Drains Template
- Hypothesis Generation Template

INDEX

Page numbers followed by *f* indicate figures.

Index

Index

Experts, assembling team of, 68–69
Extroverts, 113–115

Failure, recovery from, 39–44
Fear:
  of failure, 40
  and negativity bias, 158
  of the unknown, 183–189
Fear mitigation, "winning the day"
  and, 195–196
Feedback. *See also* 360-degree
  feedback process
  constructive, 160–161
  in education vs.
    professional world, 68
  Positive Psychology and, 127–129
Floyd, George, 93
Focus, 43–44
FOMO (fear of missing out), 75–77
Football, 20–21, 172
Framing:
  Game Plan vs. development
    plan, 170–171
  and strength-based
    approach, 132, 194
  training and, 110
Frankl, Viktor, 100–101, 184
Fulfillment/fulfilled life, winning
  and, 21–22

Gallup employee engagement
  study, 8–9
Game Plan:
  as back-and-forth process,
    176–177
  creating your own, 164–179
  embracing challenges when
    executing, 206–207
  executing, 182–202
  length of, 177
  for Pete Moore, 178–179
  organization of, 164–170
  sharing the draft with
    stakeholders, 173–175
Game Plan System (GPS), 20–34
  basics, 7–8
  in coaching process, 108–109
  consequence in, 168–169
  and constructive feedback, 161
  endpoints in, 167–168

football analogy for, 20–21
Game Plan vs. development
  plan, 170–173
goals, 164, 166–167
highway/guardrails analogy, 104
importance of printing/
  laminating, 71, 201
inner workings, 21–27
for modest goals, 207–208
and positive visualization, 30–31
sample, 25*f,* 165*f*
Gwen Sidely and, 200–202
as synthesis of ACHIEVE Model™
  elements, 209
traditional goal-setting vs., 27–31
vision articulated in, 167
visualization of conclusion, 168
"why" as unifying force, 199
as written document, 24–26
Gestalt, 82, 166
"Getting your head in the
  game," 43–44
Goals:
  ACHIEVE Model™, 169*f*
  articulated in Game Plan System,
    164, 166–167
  careful choice of, 72–73
  completing/creating new, 196–200
  developing new, 199
  in Game Plan document, 164
  and Game Plan iteration
    process, 176–177
  integration of, 166
  meaningfulness vs.
    achievement of, 151
  modest, 207–208
  nonintegrated, 167
  sharing, 70–71
  winning the day, 73–75
Goal setting:
  and "could" vs. "should," 155, 208
  deficiencies of traditional
    approach, 29–31
  GPS vs. traditional
    approach to, 27–31
  and insufficient for change, 6
  visualization and, 30–31
Goodall, Ashley, 128–129
Goodman, Diane, 76–77
Google, 107

Index

Index

Success:
  celebrating, 67–68
  defining, 51–52
  as disconnected from personal
    satisfaction, 2, 8–18
  and impostor syndrome, 129–130
  as incomplete account of road to
    achievement, 39
  and "quiet desperation," 146, 204
  and self-doubt, 185
  strategies for (*see* ACHIEVE
    Model™)
  visualization of, 188–189
  and winning the day, 195–196
Supportive environment, 69–70

Talent development, coaching for, 107
Teams:
  assembling team of experts, 68–69
  getting to think bigger, 200–202
  preserving culture as you grow,
    16–18, 113–115
Team of experts, assembling, 68–69
Therapy:
  coaching vs., 97–102
  as complement to
    coaching, 100–101
  and patient's past, 97–98
Thoreau, Henry David, 2, 4, 99
360-degree feedback process, 130–133
  and constructive feedback, 161
  interview guide for, 132–133
  for Pete Moore, 178–179
Trauma, 98–99
Triangle, why/what/how as, 205

Uncertainty, 207

Values, "should"'s compatibility
  with, 149–150
Values in Action Inventory of
  Strengths, 67, 127
Victory, as insufficient for fulfilled
  life, 21–22
Vision. *See also* "What"
  ambiguity in, 81

evolution of, 85
in Game Plan System, 167
and mental attitude, 187
symbiosis with
  consequence, 188–189
and What, Why, How model, 91
Visualization:
  of change, 187–189
  of conclusion in Game Plan
    System, 168
  and goal-setting, 30–31
  as North Star, 148
Voice of reason, 156–159

What, Why, How model, 33–34,
  58–77, 58*f*
  for finding your Piano Man, 89–92
  "how" element, 65–75
  "sources and drains" exercise,
    63–64, 63*f*
  symbiosis between elements of, 91
  "what" element, 59–61
  "why" element, 61–65
"What," 59–61. *See also* vision
"Why," 61–65. *See also*
  consequence; mission
  and could/should distinction, 169
  deficiency in SMART goal setting
    program, 205–206
  and developing new goals, 199
  difficulty of defining for successful
    businesspeople, 23
  importance to GPS, 23
  and journey to self-
    actualization, 80–85
  shifting from "how" when client
    isn't making progress, 192
  as starting point, 61
Winning:
  as distraction from true source of
    happiness, 151
  as insufficient for fulfilled
    life, 21–22
Winning the day, 73–75, 195–196
Workplace diversity, 92–94
Written document, GPS as, 24–26